FLOATING SCHOOLS & FROZEN INKWELLS

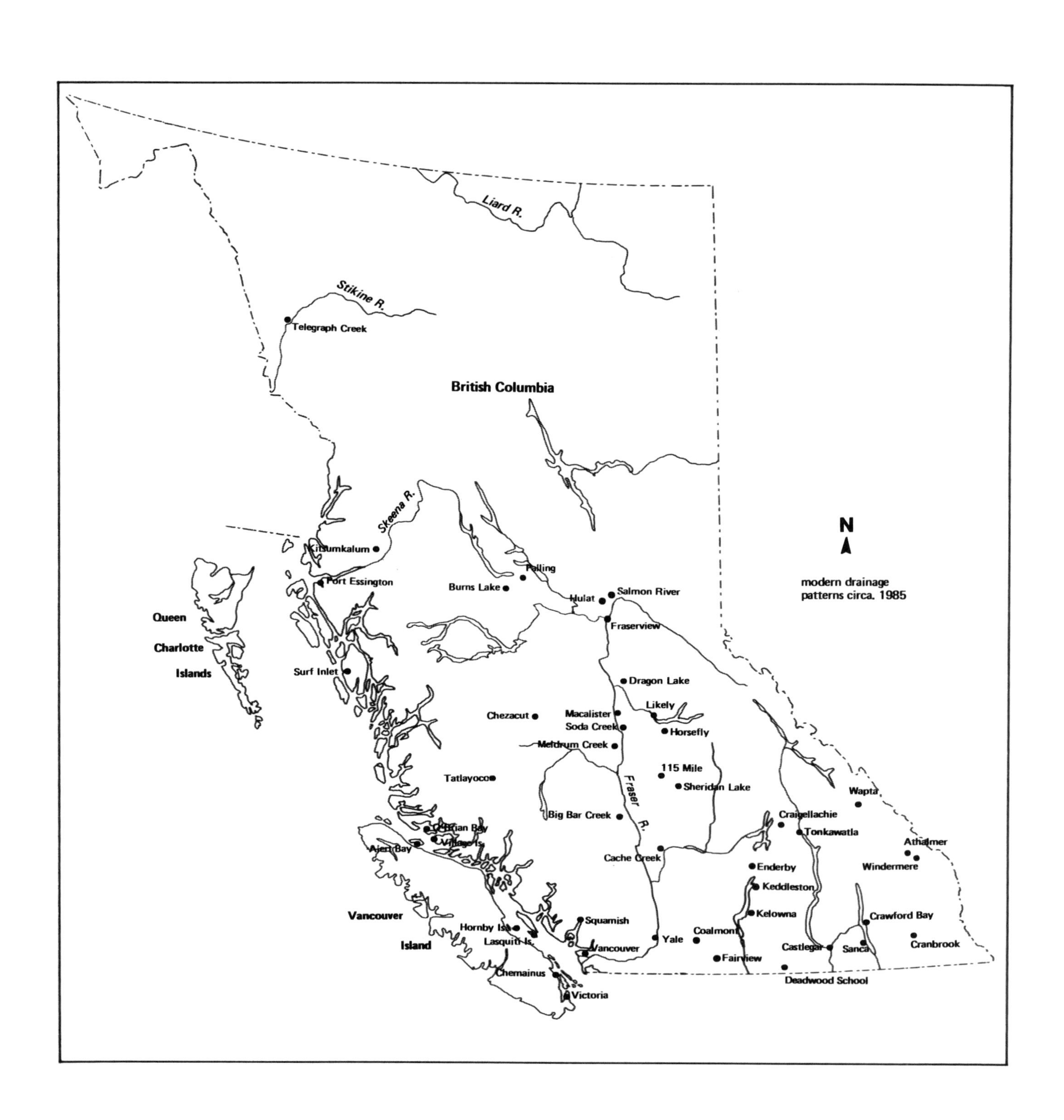
Liard R.
Stikine R.
Telegraph Creek
British Columbia
Skeena R.
Kitsumkalum
Port Essington
Palling
Burns Lake
Hulat
Salmon River
Fraserview
N
modern drainage
patterns circa. 1985
Queen
Charlotte
Islands
Surf Inlet
Dragon Lake
Chezacut
Macalister
Soda Creek
Likely
Horsefly
Meldrum Creek
115 Mile
Sheridan Lake
Tatlayoco
Fraser R.
Big Bar Creek
Wapta
Craigellachie
Tonkawatla
Athalmer
Windermere
Cache Creek
Enderby
Keddleston
Kelowna
Crawford Bay
Cranbrook
Vancouver
Island
Hornby Is.
Lasquiti Is.
Squamish
Vancouver
Yale
Coalmont
Fairview
Castlegar
Sanca
Deadwood School
Chemainus
Victoria

FLOATING SCHOOLS & FROZEN INKWELLS

The One-Room Schools of British Columbia

HARBOUR PUBLISHING CO. LTD
1985

Canadian Cataloguing in Publication Data

Adams, Joan, 1916-
Tiger

ISBN 0-920080-69-3

1. Rural schools-British Columbia-History.
2. British Columbia-Rural conditions-History.
I. Thomas, Becky, 1916 - II. Title.
LB1568.C3A32 1985 370.19′346′09711
C85-091484-1

Second Printing, 1991
Jacket design by Ian Bateson
Jacket photograph by Chris Czartoryski
Design by Gaye Hammond

Photograph credits:
British Columbia Provincial Archives, pages 10, 14, 28, 29(A), 37, 38, 45, 47, 63, 65, 69,, 84, 131; Vancouver Public Library Historical Photograph Collection, pages 11(A), 32, 33, 78, 93, 94, 109, 116, 135; J.B. Collinson, pages 70, 121(A); Ida Higgs, pages 118, 128, 140; Bernice Lawson, pages 75, 121(B), 122; Clara Lee, page 81; Lester Peterson, pages 120, 124, 125(B), 142; Pauline Romaine, pages 113, 115, 127; Kelowna Museum, page 147. Photographs not listed above collected by the authors with the kind assistance of Mary Cullum, J. Macalister, Clara Graham, Don Smith, Gilbert Yard and Don Hogarth among others. Grateful acknowledgement is made to all of the above.

Preface & Acknowledgements

Over the past few years, interest in the early history of British Columbia has increased. Heritage groups and historical societies have been formed to record and preserve this history. But the story of B.C.'s pioneer teachers and rural schools has, until now, been ignored.

It was with this thought in mind that we began interviewing teachers from British Columbia's one-room schools, in 1979. The Sound and Moving Image Division of the Victoria Archives expressed interest in adding to its collection the hundred or more tapes which resulted from these interviews.

Having gathered all this material, we decided to write the story of B.C.'s one-room schools. In doing so, we do not attempt to cover the history, sociology, or philosophy of education in B.C. We feel frankly nostalgic about our subject, and we wish to recapture something of that pioneer era and to keep its story alive for generations to come. In the past there is a solidarity and a certainty. In the future there is an unknown adventure. The everyday events of the past, however, become the folklore of the future. We hope that people of all ages will enjoy the stories of B.C.'s early teachers.

Credits and Acknowledgements

To the staff of the Sound and Moving Image Division of the B.C. Archives, particularly Mr. Derek Reimer, who encouraged us to research the history of B.C.'s one-room schools and to interview one-room school teachers throughout British Columbia.

To the Canada Council for their assistance.

To the B.C. Heritage Trust for their assistance.

To the B.C. Archives for access to their files and information, and for permission to use photographs from their collection.

To the Okanagan Historical Society for the use of material on Anthony Walsh, the first school on the August Gillard property, Frank Buckland's story of Angus McKenzie's arrival at Mission Valley, and the material about Kelowna's first school teacher, D.W. Sutherland.

To the former pupils of one-room schools who shared their memories with us.

To the teachers of one-room schools whom we interviewed and who gave so generously of their time and knowledge. Although the names of many of the teachers who helped us do not appear in this book, all contributed invaluably, for without their assistance, the story of B.C.'s one-room schools would not have been complete.

To the Doukhobor people who helped us with their history.

Table of Contents

The Rise and Fall of the One-Room School

Five decades ago, one could travel almost anywhere through the vast and lonely hinterland of British Columbia and come upon a one-room schoolhouse. Often it was a little sod-roofed log cabin nestled in a small clearing in the jackpines, or a tiny rectangular building standing isolated on a wind-swept hilltop. Very few signs of habitation would be in evidence, but somewhere in the area, on distant ranches or on small farms in the bush, there would have to be families with enough children to establish a school. Ten was the minimum enrollment required by the Department of Education in those days.

In 1932, the peak year, there were 704 one-room schools in British Columbia, each with its own school board composed of three elected trustees. Today the one-room school has become a rarity.

Hundreds of these little schools have been built and abandoned over the years since the first formal school was opened in 1849. This first school was held in Bachelor's Hall, the large dining room of the Hudson's Bay Fort, which was located near the corner of Fort and Douglas Streets in today's downtown Victoria. This school is long gone, but Craigflower School, which opened in Victoria in 1855, still stands—a tiny colonial schoolhouse of pristine white clapboard, a miracle of preservation.

We have come full circle. In 1872 there were almost as many one-room schools as there are today: ten on Vancouver Island and ten on the mainland, at Burrard Inlet, Langley, Chilliwack, Hope, Yale, Sumas, Lillooet, Lytton, Clinton, and Cariboo. At that time a Public Schools Act was passed establishing free, non-sectarian public schools open to all children from six to sixteen years of age.

John Jessop, the first superintendent of schools under this act, was greatly concerned with the problem of providing schooling for the children of the settlers who were rapidly moving into the ranching, logging, and mining communities in the vast interior of B.C. There were now hundreds living beyond the reach of education. Jessop travelled thousands of miles, organizing new schools in pioneer areas. He also had to close schools in areas where the timber supply for a sawmill had run out, or where a mine had closed and the population had dwindled away.

In the areas between settlements with schools, the families were widely scattered and it was impossible to collect the required number of children to form a school. There were six children between Lytton and Lillooet, six or seven at Big Bar Creek, and nine at Dog Creek. Alkalai Lake, eighteen miles away, had four, and on the opposite side of the Fraser there were three. At Chimney Creek and Williams Lake there were eight or nine more. At Deep Creek, Soda Creek, Mud Lake, and near old Fort Alexander, there were three or four families and seven or eight children of school age; at Quesnelmouth there were eight; at Barkerville, nine. Down the wagon road to Cache Creek, families with two or three children were to be found, from four to twenty miles apart. Along the valley there were eleven children, and at Clinton, just after the completion of the schoolhouse, two families moved away. There were nearly one hundred children, spread over an area of ten thousand square miles: about one child to a hundred square miles.

In an attempt to provide these children with education, a boarding school was opened at the junction of Cache Creek and the Bonaparte River in 1874. In spite of a stormy career, and some scandals having to do with inadequate supervision of the girls' and boys' dormitories, it carried on until 1890, by which time there were many small schools relieving the long lonely stretches.

The rapid increase of one-room schools in B.C. is linked with the development and settlement of the country. The biggest changes occurred because of transportation. In 1896, there was a sudden rise in school enrollment after the completion of the transcontinental railway. The need for a link to the interior gold fields sparked the building of the Cariboo wagon road, opening up the Cariboo and Chilcotin ranching areas to settlers. Paddle wheelers played a large part in the development of B.C. The Fraser, Thompson, Columbia, Skeena, Stikine, and Peace were all made

Read Island School, Surge Narrows, 1927.

accessible to settlers by these shallow draft river boats.

The Northern Alberta Railway line helped bring homesteaders to the Peace River country, but the vast area of north central B.C., north of the Cariboo gold fields and south of the fur trading routes, was slow to develop. The first settlers came in by pack horse from Bella Coola, a rugged three week trip, or by river boat, up the Skeena to Hazelton. They found the land heavily forested with lodge pole pine which was difficult to clear. With the completion of the Grand Trunk Pacific Railway in 1914, people began to arrive in greater numbers, lured by advertisements promising rich, banana-belt farm land. These farmers eked out their living by cutting ties for the railway, initiating the "stump farmer's" hewn tie industry, which helped settlers survive the depression years.

As families moved to these remote areas, others were bound to follow. The children were small at first, so the absence of a school was not a problem, but after a few years rolled by the three-year-old and five-year-old would be six and eight years old, and growing up without book knowledge. The arrival of new settlers with children was very important, as ten was the magic number needed to petition for a school. Sometimes even four-year-olds were hustled off to school to make up the required number, or children might be "borrowed" from a neighbour miles away and boarded in the district.

When the site was chosen for a school, the financial aspect had to be considered. "Interested persons" were responsible for footing the bill for the new school, assisted by the government. This assistance was often extremely modest. In Chezacut, for example, the government donated $125 towards the construction of a school in 1926. New school buildings could not be elaborate. In the absence of a local sawmill, the school was constructed of logs, with dimensions seldom exceeding sixteen by twenty-four feet. The

Otter Point School.

School 'bus' at Summerland.

standard pattern consisted of a small vestibule leading to an oblong room with windows down one side and a blackboard on the front wall. Children's desks were usually arranged in rows and fastened to strips of two-by-four so that they could be moved quickly when a dance was planned. In the very early days these desks and benches were hand-hewn, and the blackboard was simply a piece of painted wood. Despite the primitive conditions in these early schools, they were very important to the families which surrounded them, for the school was the centre of the community.

As time passed, the first small school often became inadequate, and a new, larger school would be built, the cost borne jointly by the Department of Education and the local school district. The new school was often in marked contrast to its little log predecessor. If there was a sawmill in the district, a smart frame building with a coat of fresh paint, usually white, was built. Sometimes a second classroom was added and another teacher hired, signalling the end of the one-room school in that district.

After the peak year of 1932, the numbers of small rural schools gradually declined, and many communities were never the same again. Roads were improved, and as cars and busses became more numerous, it seemed impractical for the government to support several little schools placed only eight or ten miles apart. Consolidation began as bussing became the practical solution to the rural school problem.

Often the parents and children in rural areas would resent the removal of their time-honoured school, stolen from them by Victoria. Letters of protest would pour in, but to no avail. Many of these small communities disappeared altogether, absorbed into larger towns and settlements.

The once-upon-a-time school of Keddleston, seven miles from Vernon on the Silver Star Road, presents a typical example of a one-room school which was once the hub of a community. In 1900, Keddleston seemed very remote indeed, separated from Vernon by a steep and winding road that was no better than a cow trail. Then settlers began to

Chezacut School, 1931.

preempt the surrounding land. Mr. and Mrs. McClusky arrived with their eight children to manage the old B.X. Ranch. Next, the Howden family moved in with their eight children. After the arrival of two other families with children, Mr. Meikin, a shy bachelor who loved children, saw the need for a school and donated a portion of his preemption for the purpose. The settlers combined their efforts, erected a small log building, and applied to Victoria for assistance in paying the teacher's salary. Keddleston School District was formed with three trustees, sixteen children, and a teacher, Miss Ersken, who was paid fifty dollars a month.

In 1913, a government grant of $600 made it possible to erect a new frame building of board and siding, with a shingle roof and windows down both sides. There were now twenty-one pupils.

These were happy years for the little school. The settlers were optimistic, accepting the joys of rural life. After three years on their preemptions, they could now purchase their land at a dollar an acre, and build permanent homes. It was a closely-knit community, and the schoolhouse became the centre for dances, church services, and meetings. Even Vernon residents came to take part in the school activities, walking or riding up the steep seven-

The La Bounty family setting off to Ten Mile School, 1932.

mile trail. The presence of Julia Ann Asher, a warm and vital teacher, did much to enhance the friendly atmosphere.

In the 1920s, however, the community of Keddleston declined. Water was scarce and times were hard. People began to leave until, by 1926, there were only seven school-aged children left. The families living in Keddleston during these years became known as the people on "Poverty Hill."

An influx of immigrants from Europe brought the attendance up again, and in 1935 the school reopened. Things did not go as well, however, for children were running wild, teachers were hard to get, and even the school dances were spoiled by rowdy elements from Vernon.

By 1951 consolidation won favour with the Vernon District School Board, and Keddleston School was closed forever. Although the building was sold to the community for one dollar, and was used occasionally for Sunday School or meetings, it eventually fell into disrepair.

Participants in an Opportunity for Youth project repaired the little school and painted it white with a brilliant blue trim in 1974. Today it stands by the road, looking forlorn, without a hope in the world of becoming the hub of anyone's community. Keddleston is now a prosperous subdivision of the town of Vernon.

The death knell of the one-room schools was struck in 1945 when the adoption of the Cameron Report reduced the existing 830 school districts to a total of 89. The number of one-room schools continued to decrease until, in 1985, less than forty were left, many of them being movable units brought into a district to serve the temporary needs of miners, construction crews, and mill workers.

Much was gained by amalgamation, and much was lost. True, there were improved schools and equipment, elimination of duplicate services, bulk purchase of supplies, centralization of administration, more medical and dental care, and more advice and help for teachers. But what a far cry are the elementary schools of today from the one-room schools of earlier times! Contrast one of these modern factories for the moulding of the juvenile mind, with the little log building in the jackpine clearing. Consider the tiny budgets of those early schools, with their careful allotment of funds prepared by three local trustees who were sweating blood over the payment for a broken windowpane.

What has become of all the hundreds of little buildings which once were schoolhouses? Some are still intact and are used as community halls, stores, or even churches. Richlands School in the Lumby area is a freshly painted Seventh Day Adventist Church, while Springhouse School in the Cariboo serves as a Women's Institute Hall. A very few of these schools have been preserved with their contents as historical sites, such as the Carling School at Three Valley Gap Museum. The vast majority of them have collapsed back into the earth, burned to the ground, or have been moved away to act as storage barns or sheds. Occasionally one might come upon an old school in the corner of some field, or in a small clearing, vines growing over the empty windows, and grass growing down from the sod roof.

However humble and outdated some of these one-room schools seem in retrospect, surely the independent spirit of those early settlers who valued education enough to build their schools with their own hands should cause us to regret the passing of that era.

Abandoned log schoolhouse, 126 Mile.

Some Early School Teachers of British Columbia

British Columbia's first teachers, while not always suited to the task, were a strong-minded lot. Wandering pedagogues from England, Scotland, or Eastern Canada may have been considered eccentric by settlers who judged a man by his ability to swing an axe and clear land, and a woman by her ability to milk cows, grow a garden, and raise five or six children. Still, it was an adventurous longing similar to that of the pioneers, which brought these educated men and women across the seas or the continent, and into the wilds to teach settlers' children. They were true pioneers.

The very first B.C. school master was an extraordinary man called Robert Staines. He was a thirty-year-old Cambridge scholar, hired by the Hudson's Bay Company in London to teach the children of its employees at Fort Victoria.

Before leaving London, Mr. Staines took Holy Orders so he could, in effect, kill two birds with one stone. In May 1849, Reverend Staines and his wife sailed into the harbour of Fort Victoria on the bark *Columbia*. Heaven knows what the newly-arrived couple had expected, but we are told that they were shocked and disappointed when they were shown their rough and barren living quarters in the Bachelor's Hall of the old Hudson's Bay fort. In fact, their initial shock occurred as they walked down the gangplank into a sea of tidal-flat mud, and saw the grim fort with its tower and palisades surrounded by primeval forest.

Robert Finlayson, who was in charge of the fort, wrote, "It was my duty to receive the new clergyman and his wife and I felt ashamed to see the lady come ashore. We had to lay planks in the mud to get them to the fort."

Reverend Staines was uncertain-tempered, proud, and very determined. We know this from many comments in letters and documents. Robert Anderson, who attended school at the fort, writes that Staines was "disposed to be unduly severe in administering corporal punishment."

About twenty children attended school, both boys and girls. The boys lived above Bachelor's Hall in very stark, cold conditions, sharing their lodgings with rats.

Robert Staines did not confine himself to teaching the children and holding Sunday services in the mess room. With an eye to the future, he acquired a thirty-six-acre farm near Mount Tolmie and began to raise cattle and pigs. As well, he grew a large garden outside the gates of the fort which the school boys tilled and weeded. According to Captain Cooper, master of the *Columbia*, he made the rounds of this estate "on horseback in a rig that would not have done discredit to Don Quixote."

Like Don Quixote, Reverend Staines began tilting at windmills. A stubborn, independent sort of man, he objected to the land monopoly of the Hudson's Bay Company, and became embroiled, with other settlers, in a bitter quarrel with Governor James Douglas, chief Hudson's Bay factor. The latter, hot-headed and fiercely protective of the Company's monopoly, denounced Reverend Staines as a "fomenter of mischief and a preacher of sedition." He suggested that Reverend Staines should stick to teaching and preaching.

While Reverend Staines became politically involved and perpetually dissatisfied with life at the fort, his wife, who must have been a patient long-suffering character, kept the school going. She is remembered as having been much kinder than her husband, and an excellent teacher. Even Governor Douglas wondered how she could stand "the fag" of running the school. He thought she was "invaluable."

A picture of Mrs. Staines, which must have been taken in later life, shows a rather stern, dark lady in a bonnet and black dress, with a row of corkscrew curls down each side of her face. She appears worn and tired. We can only guess at the unhappy life this lady led, far from accustomed English surroundings.

Five years after the Staineses arrived in Fort Victoria, there occurred a tragedy which ended the life of British Columbia's first schoolmaster. Having taken up the cause of land reform, Reverend Staines sailed for England carrying a petition from some of the

Opposite: *Mrs. Robert Staines, B.C.'s first school ma'am, Fort Victoria, B.C., 1850.*

settlers, as well as a request for funds for the erection of an Anglican church. The vessel, the *Duchess of Lorenzo*, went down off Cape Flattery and all on board were lost.

History does not record what happened to Mrs. Staines. Perhaps she returned gratefully to England where the memory of those five years in harsh and ungracious surroundings was softened by time.

In 1952, a bronze plaque was placed on the Canadian Bank of Commerce in Victoria to commemorate the site of British Columbia's first school, and in memory of Reverend Staines and his wife.

If in the early days the profession of teaching seemed to have enlisted a fair share of eccentrics, it may only have been because the teacher was highly visible in the community. Teachers, like preachers, were beings apart, expected to set an example. In a small backwoods community, the example had better be a good one or the teacher was open to sharp criticism and ridicule.

Angus McKenzie, Scotsman from Pictou County, Nova Scotia, was a man who stood the test well. This gentlemen came walking up the Okanagan Valley with his blankets and a bundle of school books on his back. He had, in his wanderings, received a teaching certificate from the state of Kansas.

According to historian Frank Buckland, McKenzie was engaged as a teacher in the Okanagan School at Mission Valley on December 20, 1875. His salary was sixty dollars a month, and he had his meat, milk, butter, eggs, and firewood provided. Mr. Buckland describes Mr. McKenzie in this way:

"He was just the kind of man who, being appointed to a remote country school with no thought of his own advancement and with no ulterior object in view, would turn to the work in hand with diligence and understanding and give to the task of educating the children entrusted to his charge the best that was in him.

Unidentified frame schoolhouse.

"Those who knew McKenzie well say that he was a big man, standing well over six feet, and that he wore his whiskers in the style of Abraham Lincoln and had one wall eye which he always partly closed when looking at anything intently. He was a gentle, kindly man, but withal, one not to be trifled with if his temper was up.

"Sometimes when the congregation gathered at the little country schoolhouse and the minister failed to keep an appointment, Mr. McKenzie would take the service himself and always very acceptably. Men like him are the salt of the earth."

Perhaps the most appealing bit of information we have about Mr. McKenzie is that he often treated the shy backward pupils to a slice of bread and syrup on the first day of school, to gain their confidence.

The schoolmaster who taught in the old mining town of Deadwood in 1913 had quite another way of appealing to pupils on the first day. Dr. Neil Morrison of Nelson tells the story:

"We all went to school that first morning not knowing a thing about the new teacher. He had come from England having been principal of a reform school at East Barrett.

"I am sure he felt he was coming to the wild and woolly west. To show his authority on that first morning, he arrived with a bundle of switches. He walked into the room and seized the two or three biggest boys in the room and whaled the daylights out of them, without saying a word, before school even began. Then he said, 'Now if I have any trouble with any of you, you know what to expect.'

"After this teacher learned that we were just ordinary scared kids and were obedient and willing to learn, he became very different and we all came to enjoy him very much. He had an odd way about him. I remember when he wanted the beginners to come up to the front, he would say, in a very English voice, 'Come here, the Pups!'"

Early teachers were not always stern disciplinarians. For example, the first teacher at Chemainus School, back in 1883, was a fellow fresh out from England who was really more interested in cricket and rounders than the Three Rs. Naturally, Mr. Lewis was quite popular.

Historian W. Olson interviewed Billie Thomas, a former pupil at Chemainus. Although ninety-seven at the time of the interview, Thomas could remember the teacher he had when he was eight years old, and in one sentence he demolished the concept we hold of stern frontier tyrants: "Sam Lewis was too easy-going and that's probably why we didn't learn much while he was there."

Mr. Lewis must have realized he wasn't cut out to be a schoolmaster for he abandoned the profession and opened a grog shop called the Louisville Hotel, on the site of which stands the present Green Lantern.

Wapta school, 1910.

Cabin at Dragon Lake used by teacher Bill Sykes.

Another interesting misfit teacher was Allan Ellis, a corner saloon missionary from San Francisco. Packing his Bible, blankets, and banjo, Mr. Ellis set out for the wilds of British Columbia, stopping first in Victoria to obtain a temporary permit to teach school. The end of a long journey found Mr. Ellis in the small settlement of Dragon Lake, not far from Quesnel, established as the schoolmaster and boarding with the local school trustee. Mr. Ellis only lasted one school term. One of his former pupils recalls Mr. Ellis as a "religious maniac," more interested in sharing a double desk with the big girls than teaching.

After this fiasco at Dragon Lake, Allan Ellis reverted to his true profession of preaching. He held missions all through the Cariboo from Prince George to Lillooet, packing his Bible and banjo with him, but the trail grows dim and nothing more is known of the wanderings of Mr. Ellis.

Being a teacher in a backwoods settlement required a good deal of diplomacy, for many communities were divided over local issues. Taking sides often proved the downfall of the teacher who could not steer a safe path through the tangled affairs of the families he dealt with.

Joseph Irwin commenced his British Columbia teaching career in 1882. He has been called, by historian A.L. Affleck, "the terrible-tempered Joseph Irwin." The tragic story of his career, which lasted from August 1882 until his death in Nelson, British Columbia, in 1918, illustrates well that a bad temper and a lack of diplomacy could ruin the career of any teacher, however intelligent. During those years, Joseph Irwin taught in ten different schools, commencing in the wild mining and construction town of Yale.

In 1893, Irwin accepted a position at Salmon Arm. The town was booming and there were thirty-one pupils, so a new school had been built to replace the old log building. This heavy responsibility did not keep Mr. Irwin from plunging into community affairs, and in no time he was chairman of the Baseball Club, master of the Orange Lodge, and an ardent supporter of the Temperance Union. Unfortunately he extended his influence too far by meddling in the affairs of the school board. There were three local trustees, the same early settlers who had struggled to establish the school in 1890. Two of these men were related and apparently Mr. Irwin felt that new blood was needed. His interference in campaigning for a change touched a match to the fuse, and the resulting explosion reverberated through the files of the British Columbia Legislature.

The furor in the small community of Salmon Arm had elements of a comic opera. There were petitions for the dismissal of Mr. Irwin, and counter-petitions. There were accusations that a parent had assaulted Mr. Irwin on the street, and that he had unjustly and brutally strapped one of the school children. There was the case of the missing dog, later found in the trustee's well. There was the offer of ten dollars to any gentleman who would thrash the schoolteacher. Verses reflecting the views of Mr. Irwin's opponents were circulated in the neighbourhood. Parents withdrew their children from school, and the children all lined up on the side of their parents. The Methodist church members complained that Mr. Irwin left the school dirty, but he in turn complained that his switch was purposely burned by someone in the congregation, and so on.

After some sixteen letters to and fro, with reports and documents to Victoria, the Salmon Arm school board received a letter from the superintendent of schools asking them to dismiss Joseph Irwin. This the new school board refused to do until the council of public instruction declined to pay Mr. Irwin's salary beyond July 31, and Mr. Irwin had his first class teaching certificate suspended. The dispute had become the subject of a legislative hearing. The whole business was, in fact, a sad commentary on life in this pioneer settlement.

As for Mr. Irwin, he and his family left Salmon Arm in April 1896 to seek their fortunes in New Denver. Here he had a short career as a notary public until his first class certificate was restored and he resumed teaching for several years in New Denver. He then went on to teach at Pilot Bay, Hume, and Ymir in the Kootenays, but apparently his temper still flared up, for there are residents of those areas who remember his heavy hand. At fifty, Mr. Irwin gave up teaching to become a freight clerk in Nelson, but the shortage of teachers during World War I caused him to embark on another three years of teaching among the peaceful Doukhobors at Perry Siding. His death in Nelson in 1918 brought to an end the turbulent career of this intelligent but hot-headed man.

Some early British Columbia teachers, although stern disciplinarians, were remembered with a great deal of affection. Such a one was Mr. Patterson, or "Pat" as he was privately known to the pupils of Athalmer School in the Kootenays. Arthur Peake of Maple Ridge, a retired school principal, recalls this teacher from the early 1920s:

"Mr. Patterson was a little Scots fellow who had served his time as an apprentice teacher in the Highlands of Scotland. He was short, broad-shouldered, round-headed with curly, thick brown hair; a little bull of a man with a lot of power in him.

"Mr. Patterson was a scholar and an excellent teacher, but what a temper! He had the Glasgow dialect and he rolled his rrr's, but despite this, it was easy to hear and interpret because he spoke so loudly and directly that you didn't dare not hear. He felt that if he shouted loud enough and hit hard enough, you would then understand. I think that worked out. I think there was some virtue in that.

"He had only one punishment—a ruler over the knuckles—and he hit really hard. If you got two mistakes in spelling, you got two good clouts.

"Every day Mr. Patterson would send us up to the blackboard, and we had to add great columns of figures, as fast as his fingers could move to the next digit. Unless we could come up with the right answer, we were in trouble. Then he would set up a list of facts—for example, the coastline waters of Europe—and you had to have the Adriatic, for instance, in the right spot. He would come with a chip on his shoulder, and if you made the slightest slip, he was right on you. The only ones who were immune in the school were the girls and they were the worst things we had. They carried home tales and embroidered on the tales.

"Notwithstanding this, he was an excellent

Clara Barkley (Graham), pioneer Kootenay teacher.

fellow, and despite his temper, he was very interesting. He told us great stories, especially about the ancient history of Scotland and the clans. He divided the world into two parts, Scots and others.

"Mr. Patterson was very well liked. You did know that if 'Pat' said he'd do something, he did it. His family lived near a lake on a little bit of a ranch, and he raised all the food they needed. I used to go over there quite often on weekends. In spite of the fact that he might have been giving a strapping the last thing before I got in his wagon, I'd go over there for the weekend, happy as a lark."

Surely one of the most gallant and adventurous of early women teachers was Clara Barkley. At the age of ninety-two Clara commented on the frequent moves she made during her eight years of teaching in Kootenay schools. "Well, you know," she said gaily, "we teachers were like gypsies in those days. We were bettering ourselves and seeing the world."

Born in 1888 of hard-working parents on a Manitoba farm, Clara moved with them to a homestead in the Beaver Valley, about twenty miles east of Trail. Her teaching career began in 1908. A one-roomed school had opened at Castlegar, sixty miles from Beaver Valley, and although Clara was untrained, she got the job. The salary was fifty dollars a month.

By Christmas in that first year of teaching, Clara realized that she would never save enough for Normal School at that rate, so she moved to Windermere in January. The salary was sixty dollars a month.

1909 found Clara teaching in the settlement

of Wapta in the Upper Columbia Valley. There was no train, only the weekly stage in winter, and in summer the steamboat on the river. In her memoirs, Clara talks of the isolation, the deep snow, and the lack of communication between the settlers. Snow sifted through the roof of the school and soot sifted through the broken stovepipes. The school board quarreled and parents took sides. It was a turbulent year, but Clara felt lucky as she was boarding at Johnson's Stopping Place, a big, clean log house run by a Swedish lady and her Irish husband. The food was good—pork in all its forms, home-grown vegetables, and ling caught in the river. Above the main floor were the curtained-off rooms for guests, with factory-cotton for walls. Each curtained room had a pitcher, jug, lamp, and chamber pot. At night, the shadows on the curtains left few secrets.

The next year Clara moved to Horse Creek, and here she bought a pony. This pony was to lead to one of her great adventures. In July 1910, not wanting to leave her pony behind, she decided to ride back to Beaver Valley, a very unusual feat for a lone woman, but Clara Barkley was no usual woman. Somehow she managed, in very restricted surroundings, to savour the drama and humour of life as would a world traveller.

The first stage of the horseback journey, Golden to Windermere, was beautiful but extremely hot; then on to Thunder Hill the next day, twenty-five miles south. After crossing the river at Canal Flat, Clara had some uneasy moments for the trail forked three ways and all the trails were unmarked. After one false start, she picked another trail and hoped for the best until, at last, a solitary man came walking towards her on the grassy side of the road, his shoes slung over his shoulder. He assured her that the stage had passed him. That night she slept at Sheep Creek and the next day, in brilliant sunshine, went on to Fort Steele. Whole families of Shuswap Indians passed Clara on the trail in horse-drawn wagons, with dogs running behind.

From Cranbrook to Nelson, both Clara and

Pupils of Clara Barkley at Ainsworth School, c. 1916.

Clara Barkley's school at Kingsgate, 1910.

the horse travelled by train, but then it was back on the trail again, or rather, back on the track, for there was no trail. Riding a horse along railway tracks can be hazardous. Clara's horse was frightened of bridges so she had to lead him down into the steep gullies and back up to the tracks. Then there was the ordeal of a forest fire burning on both sides of the track. Most frightening of all was the anticipation of the approach of the north-bound passenger train. Before each long corner, she got off her horse and held her ear to the ground before riding on. Finally the Great Northern came whistling along the track, slowing down to let Clara and her horse pull to one side. That night they reached Beaver Valley and the long ride was over.

Clara Barkley taught one more year at Windermere before she was finally able to attend Normal School and accomplish her goal: a teaching certificate. Then, while teaching for a short time in the old mining town of Yale, Clara had another adventure. When, as an old lady, she remembered this exploit, her eyes lit up with the humour of the situation, and one could visualize her as a young woman, curious, determined, and full of deviltry.

It was a Saturday, and Clara and a girlfriend who taught at the Mission School were exploring along the banks of the Fraser River. There were mining claims on the east side, and these claims could be reached by means of a "basket ferry," a wire cable from which was slung a rough wooden platform. Pack horses for the mine went over in this sling. It occurred to Clara that she had never been on the other side of the Fraser River. The temptation was too much, so tucking up her long skirts, she climbed onto the basket ferry and began pulling herself over. Half way across the cable stuck, and there she was, precariously balanced and hopefully tugging, while below the mighty Fraser eddied and swirled. Fortunately for her, some men came by on the east side of the river and, seeing her plight, pulled her across.

The student body of Erie School. Clara Barkley, teacher.

Clara Barkley taught in three more one-room schools before she met and married CPR train engineer Percy Graham, in Cranbrook. Her questing, romantic spirit did not allow her to bury herself in household tasks, however. She went on to write four extraordinarily vivid books about the history of the Kootenays, the last of which, *Kootenay Yesterdays*, was written in her eighties. To read these accounts is to relive the era.

In her nineties, Clara Graham recalled for the writers a poem which she had learned as a small child in a rural school. The poem, although simple and moralistic to suit the tone of the day, seems to sum up the steadfast courage and spirit of so many of British Columbia's early teachers, few of whom have left written records of their experiences:

Never give up! 'Tis the secret of glory.
Nothing so wise can philosophy preach.
Look at the lives that are famous in story
Never give up,
'tis the lesson they teach.
How have men compassed immortal
achievements,
How have they molded the world to
their will?
'Tis that midst trials and sorest
bereavements
Never give up, was their principle still!

Schools Usual & Unusual

There really was no blueprint for a typical British Columbia one-room school. Over the past hundred years, however, three distinct types of buildings evolved, the most appealing and romantic of which was certainly the log school house.

The independence which characterized the lives of early settlers was exemplified by these early schools, for their logs were skidded out of the bush by the fathers of the children who used the schools. Whether they were simply peeled and left in the round, or hewn flat with a broad axe, the logs served their purpose well; the spaces between them were snugly fitted with peeled saplings, or stuffed with moss or mud, and the corners were saddle-notched the easy way, or dove-tailed by an experienced axeman. The floor of the school was usually of whip-sawn planks, but if milled lumber was available, the inside walls and the ceiling might be finished off with boards.

The roof-poles of log buildings were often covered with cedar shakes or, in the dry Interior, with sod. Over time, the shake roofs became green with lichen or moss, while the sod roofs supported a crop of weeds, grass, and daisies. The logs greyed and weathered so that the whole effect was friendly and natural. The little buildings seemed a part of the landscape.

Teacherage with sod roof and dirt floor, Big Bar Creek, 1931.

Series showing details of Robin's Range School near Kamloops. In 1985 the hewn log structure was laboriously dismantled and removed to Kamloops, where it was reassembled on the grounds of Pineridge Elementary School.

Operated from 1915 to 1956 in a logging area above Kamloops, Robin's Range School was preserved as a centennial project commemorating 100 years of schooling in the Kamloops area. It survives as a combined museum and classroom.

Abandoned school at Big Creek, Chilcotin.

Some early log schools do survive, especially if kept in repair, but the rotting of the foundation logs is usually the downfall of these buildings. At Big Creek, in Chilcotin country, a dilapidated log structure stands in a clearing. Local people say this was once the Big Creek School but this is very hard to imagine as the logs have settled to such an extent that the door seems too low for any grown person to use. Anyone curious enough to peer in this door will see, amidst the rotting logs, the skeleton of a long-dead horse.

Log schools went out of style and were gradually supplanted by frame schools, particularly in areas where there was a local sawmill. The frame school was a simple oblong structure with a steep shingle roof, a cloakroom built on the front, and a small porch with two or three steps. Sometimes there were four or five windows down both sides; an arrangement which made for poor cross-lighting. Painted white with a trim, these schools had a neat, prim appearance, not unlike the rural churches of the same era, but

Old school near Falkland.

when the paint wore off, the steps sagged, and the outhouses leaned to one side, these buildings were not as picturesque as their predecessors.

Until recently, a bleak example of a frame school in disrepair stood by the roadside near the village of Falkland. It was especially notable because across one side of the school, either in jest or in earnest, someone had boldly painted, "Jesus Christ Please Help Us!" The passerby could imagine this as the despairing cry of some unfortunate teacher who could not squeeze enough supplies from her school board. This mournful landmark has now disappeared.

The practical modern solution to education in small outlying settlements, construction sites, and road camps is the mobile trailer school. Fuelled by propane gas or oil, and equipped with electric lights and plumbing, there is no doubt that the trailer school offers more comfort to the teacher and pupils than the old log or frame schools ever did—that is, as long as the electric light plant works, the plumbing does not freeze, and the oil runs freely. When these fail, the teacher might think back nostalgically to the log school, with its gas lamp, drum stove, woodpile, and outhouses—so uncomplicated that nothing could go wrong (unless the roof caught on fire or a packrat got into the attic).

When the people of a community were unable to build their own schoolhouse, they often resorted to peculiar makeshifts, which they pressed into service until financial help could be secured from the government. As a result, the children of early settlers often went to school in barns, trappers' cabins, farmhouses, store-fronts, granaries, churches—even, in one case, in a tent. Of course these makeshifts were abandoned eventually in favour of real schools. In the meantime, teachers and children had to make the best of it and pin their hopes on the future. Such a situation existed in the old gold-mining town of Fairview.

Class with tent schoolhouse, Chilco, 1914.

Rose Glover, the seventeen-year-old who became Fairview's first schoolteacher in 1886, recalled years later that she cried from homesickness as she journeyed first by steamer down Okanagan Lake to Penticton, and then by stagecoach to Fairview. When she saw her school she must surely have shed more tears. On that first day, as Rose and the children walked up the dusty gulch towards the school, we are told that miners in front of the Golden Gate Hotel raised their hats to her. Well they might, for the seventeen-year-old had to open school in an abandoned miner's cabin—walls of broken rock, roof of poles, and a floor of earth. It was half cabin, half dugout, and had belonged to a miner called Billie Dalrymple.

The next year Miss Glover taught in the Fairview Anglican Church until at last, in the spring of 1888, a new school which even boasted a real blackboard, was built. The wild mining town of Fairview was becoming civilized. Today Rose Glover's new school no longer exists for the town of Fairview has disappeared.

A great many of the first schools in the Cariboo made use of log buildings that had first served more lowly purposes. Glen Walters of Horsefly remembers attending school, when he was nine, in a bunkhouse on his father's ranch. They simply took out the partitions and bunks, and put up board covered with painted cloth for blackboards. The children sat on benches. Glen claims his education did not suffer—he went on to become a successful rancher and married a schoolteacher. The log schoolhouse that succeeded the bunkhouse school in 1922 now stands empty by the side of the road.

Fairview when Rose Glover arrived to open first school in 1886.

Opposite: *Rose Glover, 17, teaching in abandoned miner's shack, Fairview, 1886.*

Below, opposite: *Old school at Horsefly.*

Phyllis Burnett opened her Cariboo school in a building which had served two uses before it was elevated to this lofty purpose.

"I had to hold school in what must at one time have been a residence, as there was a root cellar behind it and a little woodshed. It must then have been used as a barn because there were traces of animals. It had a dirt floor so a rancher came and put some planks down. Then a cowboy brought in two saw-horses and placed across the top of these some planks, and that was my desk. I had to find a cat because of the mice, and we put a cow's tail on the door to hold it shut. There was an old air-tight heater which looked as though someone had taken pot-shots at it for it was full of holes, but when the flames were shooting up, it did make a cheery corner of the room."

Two other Cariboo teachers have described the log building which served as a school at Meldrum Creek in Chilcotin ranching country. Mary Cullum, who taught there in 1931, recalls the inspector saying that it was the worst school in B.C. and looked like a root house. It was on the corner of a little ranch and is still standing there, very gloomy and dirty.

Sylvia McKay has vivid memories of this same school:

"I still remember the day I was shown the school. The fellow said, 'There's your schoolhouse. It's unlocked.' I went to the door and was greeted by a bunch of cobwebs. I pushed them aside and went in. I remember standing there and looking at the centre beam. I'm sure it has been magnified by my memory, but it was the biggest beam I've ever seen. I learned that every new teacher was given a roll of building paper and was told to paper the walls and ceiling. I, too, proceeded to do this but, of course, the paper always fell down when it rained as the building had a sod roof. There were poles, then straw, then sod, and dirt and grass.

"There were mice galore in that building. You couldn't keep anything that had glue on it. The backs of books or any work the children did with paste gave the mice a heyday. They must have been starving because we had a washbasin and bar of lifebuoy soap on a saucer, and in the morning you could picture all the mice sitting around the saucer. There were always tooth marks on the soap. I remember one of the grade ones giggling in the middle of a serious lesson. A mouse was in the folds of paper on the ceiling. As it scampered away, all the dust fell on the desks."

At a place called Dorr, in Boundary country in the East Kootenays, the school had once been a private house. It had a rather strange veranda which seemed to be a woodshed, but behind the woodshed was a trap door. One day the teacher ventured to pull up the trap

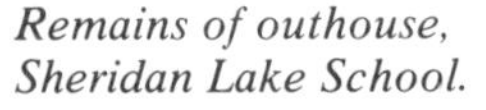

Remains of outhouse, Sheridan Lake School.

door and go part way down the steps, but she didn't care to poke around any further. Those were prohibition days and she had heard that the cellar of her school had once been used as a bootlegger's hideout.

Herbert Dodd taught at a school in the Kootenays called Sanca Flats. A new community had sprung up on the site of an old mining development. All that remained of the original settlement were the basements of some buildings and eight or ten red shacks on a hillside. One of these shacks became the school. Times were hard; so hard that it was difficult to find anyone who qualified, by paying taxes, to sit on the school board. The first desks in this school were pieces of driftwood with planks stretched across. Mr. Dodd recalls that water would freeze on the floor of the school, and those sitting farthest from the cast iron stove were very chilly indeed.

One day the manager of a fly-by-night mining company appeared at the school just at recess time and demanded the key. He claimed the school was squatting on his silver claim. Mr. Dodd staunchly refused to give up the key until he got hold of the secretary of the school board. That night there was a confrontation between the board, the inspector of schools, and the manager of the silver claim. The matter was temporarily resolved and the following year a new school was built.

It was not just the schools and their basic furnishings that were makeshift in those early days. Mr. Dodd taught at the site of another abandoned mine in the Kootenays, called Alice Siding. This school had one strange feature:

"I recall the water supply at Alice Siding. There was a well in the yard and it was the duty of one of the older boys to pump the water. In the winter, the pump would freeze and there was no way to get water. Across the road and up a steep incline about fifty yards, there was a mine shaft, really a tunnel. Some enterprising individual had put a dam at the rear end of the tunnel, which went in perhaps a hundred feet, and this held back crystal clear water. With a lantern, you could go in and dip out two buckets at a time.

"I vividly recall it because there were bats all along the ceiling of the tunnel, and thousands and thousands of mosquitoes, big, fat fellows, hibernating. I think the tunnel was originally a lead-zinc showing and I've often wondered what the lead content of the water was!"

Malcolm McPhee taught at the same school and has similar memories of rats scurrying out of the tunnel. He observes that teacher, children, and rats shared the same drinking water, but no harm seemed to come to any of them.

Conditions at Soda Creek were not much better, according to the teacher, Edith Money. The water supply for her school came from a farmer's creek, and many a time the water can had tadpoles in it.

Some Peace River school boards solved the problem of suitable drinking water with an

Joe Murray's trapping cabin-cum-schoolhouse, Chilco. Below: *Two-holer in ruins, 126 Mile.*

icehouse. The parents would cut ice on a river or lake and haul it to the icehouse for storage. A bigger boy would have the responsibility of bringing in a block of ice, cleaning the sawdust off, and putting it in the icebarrel to melt.

At the back of every school room was a bench for the water pail and wash basin. In pioneer days, one dipper or cup served all, for crockery was scarce and no one worried about germs. Public Health nurses, however, were very keen on germs, and by the thirties there were rows of labelled cups over the water pail.

The primitive source of comfort, and the most prominent feature in most of the log and frame schools, was the drum stove or barrel heater. Around this monster, which could take four-foot lengths of wood, revolved the day's activities for at least seven months of the year. The desks moved towards the heater in the morning, and the other way as the day progressed, as children roasted on one side and froze on the other. In winter, rows of mittens and scarves festooned the metal guard at the back of the stove, and boots, moccasins, and German rubbers lined up around it, so that the odour of damp wool mingled with the smell of singeing rubber, moosehide, and wood smoke. On especially cold days the teacher let the children sit up close to the stove on sticks of wood, their mitts and coats still on,

Eburne School showing interior, c. 1900.

and sometimes at noon there would be a pot of good hot soup on top of the stove.

Cutting shavings to start the next day's fire was somewhat of a ritual with older boys who possessed hunting knives. A piece of wood with a good smooth grain was held with the end against the boy's stomach while he slowly drew his sharp knife towards himself, and turned the stick. The ability to cut nicely-curled shavings was an art.

Pupils of early schools sat on wooden benches in front of handmade double desks. Later desks were ordered from the Department of Education. They came in three sizes: small (no.5), medium (no.3), and large (no.2), and were nailed down by their metal legs in a series, on two-by-fours, so that five or six had to be moved at once. Matching the desks and the pupils could present a problem. Sometimes a child outgrew one size, but found his chin resting on the desk of the next bigger series.

Bowen Island School, c. 1900.

Basic equipment, apart from the paper supplies and text books kept in the storage cupboards at the back, was very simple in the early one-room schools. It was not unusual for blackboards to be made of tar paper or of boards painted green or black. Real slate blackboards which covered at least one wall were every teacher's dream, for blackboards helped to organize the day's work. Along the blackboard ledge were the red-white-and-blue chalk brushes, a large wooden compass, and a wooden pointer, while above the blackboard were several pull-down maps becoming more tattered as the years went by—usually one of North America and one of the World.

Somewhere in the back cupboard there was sure to be a stark white wooden ball, a triangle, a cone, and a square. These objects were intended for Friday afternoon drawing lessons. After struggling to render them in three dimensions on manila drawing paper, the pupils could then look forward to drawing and shading the teacher's coffeepot or an apple from someone's lunch pail.

Some lucky schools boasted an organ, as church was often held in the schoolhouse, but these schools were in the minority. The teacher, compelled to teach singing even if tone-deaf, had usually to rely on a pitch pipe.

Raising the flag at Bearhead School near Vanderhoof, 1923.

Very few schools had clocks, but most had a picture of the reigning monarch—or one that had ceased to reign. Betty Patterson taught at Hornby Island in 1921 in the original log school. She remembers the inspector's first visit and his surprise at finding Queen Victoria presiding over the classroom. "Well, my goodness! You're not up to date. Look, you've got Queen Victoria up there. We've had King Edward in the meantime. Can't you get one of George the Fifth?"

A young and enthusiastic teacher was usually proud of the school for, after cleaning it up, perhaps putting curtains at the windows and pictures on the walls, or constructing extra furniture from orange and apple boxes, it began to look like home. Some teachers had the children plant gardens and outline them with stones, but the gardens, of course, withered in the summer months and were not really practical.

A description of the one-room school would not be complete without some mention of the Union Jack and the flagpole. It was certain that wherever there were English settlers, the flag would be hoisted up the pole at the beginning of every school day. Patriotic teachers even had their pupils line up and stand to attention before marching in to school. The sight of the Union Jack flying from the pole gave the school, however rough and primitive, authority and dignity.

The one-room school of today bears little resemblance to its earlier counterpart. Whether housed in a double-wide trailer, or in a frame building, the modern school offers sophisticated teaching equipment such as t.v., video slide projector, record player, duplicator, and possibly a recording station. There are ample shelves for a large library, and the walls are covered with bright charts and learning aids. Some schools even have a bus for field trips.

Lesley Newman became a schoolteacher at Chezacut in 1967. To reach this remote settlement one drives ninety-seven miles west of Williams Lake to Redstone, then thirty-five miles north on a narrow rutted road. This is sparsely populated rolling rangeland country. Here Mr. Newman, who had previously taught in a very primitive school in South Africa, witnessed the changeover from the original back-country log school to a modern self-sufficient double-wide trailer.

"The school was built entirely of logs and it was very old. I convinced Mr. Flowers, the superintendent, that if he didn't give me a new school within a year or so I would not be responsible if the roof caved in on us. That gave him an excellent excuse and we had a new school.

"A double portable was dragged in and from that time our school was really upgraded. We had a well drilled, and a little propane generator for electricity. Then we had indoor plumbing. It was very strange. I thought these children would really make a mess when we had indoor plumbing and hot and cold running water, but I was really impressed by how they behaved. They kept it absolutely spotlessly clean.

"The children had the facilities of films, a projector and a listening station which I set up and wired, headsets, record player, and tape recorder. It was fantastic how quickly children who had never used or seen electricity picked it up. They were capable of plugging in and transferring from a record player to a tape recorder, and even cross-wiring the looser wires. In a month they were absolutely familiar with it—rancher's children and little Indian children."

Everything changes, even Chezacut. The road has been widened for logging trucks, and civilization begins to encroach. Perhaps it is just as well that the children have learned to deal with electrical equipment and flush plumbing. There are some teachers, however, who cast a backward, nostalgic look at the earlier one-room schools.

Lorna Woodman was teaching in 1978 in the very modern trailer school in the ranching district of Big Creek. Although she and her small class of ranchers' children enjoyed every convenience in their cheerful, bright classroom, Lorna, a romantic young person, seemed nostalgic for the old days of the log school. She commented, "Not everyone can go and live in the country and be at ease, especially if you're isolated, but I often think how it was in the early days. Here I am with hydro, telephone, furnace, and running water. I would love to have gone through that era of packing water, of outdoor toilets, and the wood stove."

Above: One-room school, 1978 style, Big Creek. Teacher, Lorna Woodman. 1978. Below: Big Creek schoolhouse may have modern conveniences, but pupils still come on horses.

There are very few one-room schools left in the remoter areas of British Columbia, and all of these have been modernized to some extent. Gone are the days when country children rarely went on to high school, when parents were satisfied if a child could read and write well enough to fill out an order to Eaton's catalogue. There is real concern now to offer equal opportunities to children wherever they may be.

Times have changed, but today's one-room schools still have one thing in common with the schools of yesteryear: their isolation.

The School ~ Hub of the Community

It is hard for us to imagine the very long shadows which humble little schools cast in the early days. It was as if the idea of the school, rather than the actual building, loomed up and took over the imaginations of early settlers. Getting together with neighbours to build a school for their children made the past struggle to establish homes in the wilderness seem worthwhile. To have a schoolhouse, however rough or small, meant that there really was a community.

This wonderful, warm feeling of optimism is described by one old-timer who recalls the settlers meeting to establish a school south of Mission Creek, near the present town of Kelowna:

"A log house, long deserted, on the old Fred Gillard property, was suggested as a makeshift for a schoolhouse. All the settlers who had families were quickly rounded up and on a sunny afternoon a meeting was held at the old shack.

"The question was, could they fix up that old decrepit cabin and provide all the school equipment necessary without outside help? The answer was a determined 'yes' from every individual present. All had hammers and saws, and they went at it with a will to succeed.

Community-built school on land donated by Robert Donley, Pender Harbour, c. 1920. Opposite: *School doubling as church, Palling, c. 1940.*

"The work was apportioned and things began to hum. The roof and chimney were repaired, uneven floors levelled, chinks between the logs were filled with mud, doors and windows appeared, rough desks and seats took shape, blackboards were made and homey touches were added by the ladies. In a couple of weeks, the school was open for business and we started with an enrollment of eighteen. The little school which started under such adverse circumstances prospered amazingly!"

Although the government usually assisted settlers to build or fix up a school by giving a very small monetary contribution, it was seldom enough to purchase more than the bare essentials. Once having put their minds to building a school, the strongest supporters usually cast about for some extra cash. Dances and box socials were good fund raisers, but only if there were a fair number of bachelors in the area. An unidentified old-timer remembers a boisterous crowd on the second floor of George McKenzie's store in Burns Lake, at a sale of ladies' lunch baskets in aid of the new school:

"The bidding ran high. The town was full of trappers and fur buyers. Some bids were as high as seventy-five dollars, to the disgust of local romeos.

"The ladies had all gathered on the dance floor, but the men adjourned to the Snake Room taking all the baskets with them. The usual aggregation of fiddlers were strumming away, and Frank Eckert, who was in great demand because of his ability with his accordion, called for a waltz. But the men were conspicuous by their absence. Sizing up the situation, the auctioneer of the baskets went over to the Snake Room and addressed the gathering as follows, 'Hey, you guys, what kind of sports do you think you are? Don't you know you only bought half interest in those baskets? Take your basket back to the girl who made it up. She is supposed to be your partner and you are responsible for her entertainment.'

"There was little argument. They gathered up the baskets and invaded the hall. The dance was a howling success, and a new school was under way."

Unfortunately, establishing a new school was not always as easy as organizing a box social. Sometimes, before a school could become the hub of a community, a lot of dust was thrown up, for so much emotion surrounded this important undertaking that there were bound to be conflicting opinions. If the exchanges were too bitter it might be some time before the dust settled and the little school became acceptable to everyone.

For example, one rancher might suggest that the school be in one corner of his meadow, while the wife of a second would propose a site close to their barn in the lower forty. A third settler, known for his thriftiness, might point out that it would be cheaper to fix up an abandoned shack farther down the road. As the storm raged, the thrifty trustee would be called a "stubborn old penny-pinching skinflint," and during their tenure as trustees, two of these people might not be on speaking terms.

Just such a struggle took place at Crawford Bay on Kootenay Lake in the early 1900s, between the immigrant English fruit ranchers who lived on one side of the creek that divided the settlement, and the Canadians who worked for them and lived on the other side. Although the children were, for the most part, from the Canadian side of the creek, as were the trustees, the English settlers sent a delegation to every meeting with the inspector, to insist that the school be on their side of the creek. According to records, the site of the school was changed five times. Crawford Bay was nicknamed "School Bay" by officials in Victoria.

A very amusing and bizarre example of "school snatching" occurred at Wistaria, in

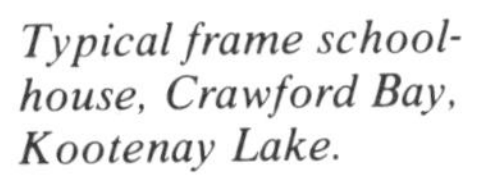
Typical frame schoolhouse, Crawford Bay, Kootenay Lake.

the Ootsa Lake district. Thanks to the peaceable nature of the parents, and the beautiful sang-froid of the children, the incident was more comic than violent. Beatrice Carroll, daughter of pioneer Bill Harrison, tells the story:

"One beautiful autumn morning we arrived at the little log schoolhouse to find no teacher, and in the schoolhouse—nothing! There were no desks; even the stove was gone.

"We played around for awhile and then meandered home. The muskatell berries were delicious. The woods, colourful. We enjoyed it so much. Upon our arrival home, we found the teacher explaining to our parents what had happened. It appeared that the night before, when he was preparing to leave the school, an irate neighbour rode up on his saddle horse carrying a rifle and demanded that the teacher load everything from the school into his wagon and transport it about a mile and a half to a vacant building where he had decided that the school should be to accommodate some of the pupils.

"'And suppose I refuse to oblige you in this outrage?'

"'Then I will force you,' said the other, patting his rifle.

"The teacher worked till late moving the school. The big man followed him. It was decided that the best thing was to do nothing, but to attend school where it now was. Actually, the distance meant nothing to us and we welcomed the new route.

"The next day we were away bright and early to the new location. Upon our arrival, we found the building completely empty, no desks, books, stove—nothing! Of course we wondered what had happened but we played happily around the new place, found some new berry patches and old birds' nests, made a picnic of our lunches and finally wandered home.

"Again, the teacher had called on my parents. He explained that when he found the school empty, he had followed the fresh wagon tracks back to the proper school. Everything had been replaced. The big man had undoubtedly decided that he had acted unwisely and had gone in the night or early morning and moved them. Again it was decided to make no fuss about it. 'The best way is the quiet way.'

"The next morning we arrived at school to find things almost in their proper places. Needless to say, we children were very disappointed that the holiday was at an end."

Lunch hour, Ootsa Lake School, 1944.

After a school was established, the Department of Education allotted money from local taxes to a three-man school board that ran the school. It was usually a pitifully small budget, as people were taxed according to their income and the settlers were very poor. Teachers sometimes had to beg for as much as an extra thumb tack, and woe betide the child who knocked a ball through the school window.

A little bit of money was very important and sometimes people lined up on two sides of the fence because of this. A resident who attended a one-room school in the Bulkley Valley recalls a time when the books of the school board were "covered with blood." It seems that a neighbour who audited the books had the bad taste to question one of the members about a figure. He was promptly punched in the nose!

Work bee breaks for lunch, Quick School, c.1920.

The secretary of the school board was the fellow in charge. He determined who, if anyone, would cut the wood, haul the water, light the fire in the morning, or scrub the school floor once a year. He also usually determined where the teacher would board.

Understandably, feelings ran high. The school was the most important institution in the community, particularly in a remote rural area, and those who controlled the school wielded the power. If feelings ran too high the Board of Education, on the advice of the school inspector, temporarily disbanded the school board and the school would be run by the inspector until the situation mellowed with time.

The use of the one-room school as the social centre in a district depended very much on the character of the community. Sometimes when settlers were of mixed racial origins, it took years for a neighbourly feeling to develop. Extreme poverty and long, lonely stretches between homesteads often meant that people would keep to themselves, especially when the temperature dropped. In some ingrown communities, feuding developed between families so that even the children played separately in the schoolgrounds. One teacher remembers the man of the house where she boarded stamping into the kitchen of the farmhouse and exhibiting a bullet hole in his hat. Later a neighbour's horse came to an untimely end.

In some areas people helped one another, enjoyed one another's company, and shared a similar sense of humour. For example, when the school in the Chezacut area needed more pupils, a bet was made which hinged on the ability of one lady to persuade a relative to buy a certain ranch and move his family closer to town. The stakes were high—a box of chocolates. The lady won the bet.

Of course the personality of the teacher was very important. Youth and energy were valuable assets, and a teacher who was fun-loving and a good mixer could stir up a lot of enjoyment during the long winter months. If the school was the hub of the community, such a teacher could be called the kingpin.

One thinks first of the Christmas concert, with its infinite variations and its overriding importance. With this event, the teacher and perhaps only eight or nine children, however humble their efforts, brought together the whole community. The following comments may serve to illustrate this:

"I remember the first year I was up there. We had a Christmas Concert. I guess it was the first one they ever had in that school. We sent out to Eaton's for little gifts for the youngsters. We sang our songs and said our pieces and gave out the presents. Several of my trustees and a few more of them had tears in their eyes. They were very appreciative."

"There wasn't much of a social life, but we did put on a Christmas Concert. There was no music. The only accompaniment was my harmonica so that's what we used. The place was packed. What else was there to do?"

"We had our Christmas Concert one year in the middle of the day. We decided, 'Let's have a dinner!' The men brought saw-horses and lumber and made a table from one corner of the school to the other. We covered it with tablecloths and there were turkeys, chickens, roasts of veal and pork, and homemade ice-cream. We had a little concert of recitations and songs and, of course, a lovely family Christmas tree—everyone together. The bachelors had nothing else to go to but that. It was a beautiful Christmas."

One bachelor teacher describes the "do it yourself or go without" kind of entertainment at a Christmas concert in his school:

"People came for miles around. As there were only eight children, several adults put on acts. The women and I put on one in which they were taking a pair of my trousers off the line. In the struggle, they tore the trousers in two. I sang, 'They go wild, simply wild over me!'"

Christmas concerts and schoolhouse dances belong to the folklore of our country. Both were entertainments of an earlier era for which there was a basic tradition but no set rules.

Imagine the tight squeeze at a schoolhouse dance—desks pushed back as far as they could go, babies stashed under them, and the musicians sweating away in a corner by the blackboard under the harsh light of a gas lamp. If the drum stove happened to be in the centre, the dancers just went around it in circular style, or made a square on either side. Sometimes the stove was taken out of the school altogether; with energetic polkas and schottisches there was no need for extra heat unless it was the dead of winter.

Agnes Smith, who taught at Sidmouth on the Columbia River, recalls a lively schoolhouse dance:

"'Swing your Partner' meant just that, right up to the ceiling. One night, a young lumberjack, in the delight of the dance, swung the one-hundred-and-five pound teacher from Hall's Landing right out the door. Unfortunately, her head struck the door jamb and she was temporarily knocked out. Those were prohibition days, but if one sniffed hard enough, the delicate aroma of home-brew could be detected."

Over the years, the music for country dances has changed. In the early days it was all reels, break-downs, two-steps, and waltzes, with tunes like "Red Wing," "My Pretty Quadroon," "Soldier's Joy," "Turkey in the Straw," and the "Spanish Waltz." Music was supplied by a catch-all combination of violin, piano, accordion, mandolin, or mouth organ, and no one played for money.

After radios became common in the early thirties, new tunes began to filter through—"Springtime in the Rockies," "Red River Valley," and "If I Had the Wings of an Angel." Later came really modern songs like "Elmer's Tune," "Don't Fence Me In," "South of the Border," and "The Tennessee Waltz." Still, no matter how catchy new tunes were, there were always some old-fashioned two-steps and squares before the dance ended.

Church was often held in the schoolhouse too, the preacher holding forth once or twice a month to a small, mixed congregation. People would squeeze into the children's desks. If there were no piano or organ, two or three could usually be counted on to carry a tune. They sang the old favourites like "Bringing in the Sheaves," "Will Your Anchor Hold in the Storms of Life?" and "The Old Rugged Cross." If it was winter, horses would be blanketed and tied up by the barn.

There were schoolhouse weddings and even schoolhouse funerals. The school was used

June 6, 1932: Hauling out stove to make room for farewell dance, Ten Mile School.

for the Cattlemen's Association, the Fishermen's Union, political meetings, card parties, amateur dramatics, concerts, the Farmers' Institute, and the Women's Institute. One male teacher, Ben Carlson, relates that he was the secretary of the Women's Institute and that it met in the schoolhouse. It seems there was a grant available from the government for a Farmers' Institute, but there were no farmers in that area, only fishermen. The men, with great expediency, teamed up with the women and they all met together as the Women's Institute to settle the community problems. The grant, ten dollars a years, paid for the stamps, envelopes, and sugar for the coffee at five cents a pound.

Mr. A.S. Towell, the inspector in the Peace River area, purchased a Marconi battery-operated radio for each school in his district. This was of tremendous importance because there were few newspapers in the homes—with the exception of the *Winnipeg Prairie Farmer*—and almost no books. Reading was curtailed in the winter anyway because of the cost of fuel for the lamps. One night each week Charles Bruce, the teacher at Upper Pine, opened his school and people came with their youngsters to listen to "Grand Old Opry." The school teacher thus provided ongoing entertainment for everyone.

Teacher Don Smith and family he boarded with in 1936, Peace River area.

In one area with a mixture of German, Russian, Polish, Yugoslavian, French, and Swiss settlers, the teacher held night school for adults who wished to learn to speak English. She did this with no thought of remuneration, but simply because she saw the need.

Male teachers were often called on in emergencies, usually in the most horrendous weather, when a pregnant lady or a sick child had to be rushed to hospital miles away. Donald Smith, who taught in the Peace River, recalls such an incident.

"A child at a neighbour's house took ill and that evening went into a coma. The following day, I closed the school and the father and I set out twenty-five miles for Dawson Creek to take the child to the hospital. The temperature was forty-five below. The transportation was a team and cutter. One sat on the sleigh tending to the child, the other ran behind, turn about. Several miles from Dawson Creek, we were met by the doctor and the child was taken to the hospital. A short time later, she returned home, normal and happy."

It goes without saying that some teachers involved themselves in the affairs of the community with better grace than others. These were the unsung heroes and heroines of the one-room school; men and women who were truly dedicated. Throughout the history of most of these schools, however, teachers came and went, sometimes in very rapid succession. In twelve years, a school might have ten teachers, some beloved, some feared and respected, and some tolerated. One of the ten might be eccentric enough to cause a scandal, but misfits usually did not last long, and went down the line to be hired by some other unfortunate school board. The school survived all the changes, and the community revolved around this much-used, much-discussed, sometimes fought-over symbol of civilization.

The Training of a Backwoods Teacher

Until quite recently, rural schools were looked upon as training grounds, where a new teacher could gain experience before moving on to teach at a school in town. This attitude had its roots in pioneer times. As one-room schools sprang up like mushrooms after rain, settlers were glad to accept as teachers the most likely candidates that turned up in their districts, many of whom had absolutely no training. The government cooperated by issuing temporary "teaching permits" to the teachers chosen by those first school boards. Sometimes this situation resulted in ridiculous extremes. A cultured Oxford graduate might be struggling to make himself understood by thirty backwoods children in one district while only a few miles away, a farm girl, not yet sixteen, was having her own troubles as she tried to impart a rudimentary knowledge of the Three Rs. For both teachers, the situation was likely to be a sort of "trial by fire."

In 1874 there were thirty-six teachers in the employ of the newly formed Department of Education. Only eight of these had any training at all, and the eight were undoubtedly imports from Great Britain, Eastern Canada, or the United States. The situation was desperate. Settlers clamoured for more schools to be opened, but where was the government to find qualified teachers? The Department of Education, in order to solve the problem and to insure some sort of standard, prepared tests for the licensing of teachers. In July 1874, thirteen candidates presented themselves for the examinations which took place in the Legislative Assembly. There were eight ladies and five gentlemen, and of these, eleven obtained a certificate.

The types of questions asked on these examinations were as varied in their categories as were the applicants themselves. There were six grades ranging from First Class A to Third

The art class.

Opposite: *Schoolhouse interior, Le Jeune.*

Class B. To obtain a First Class A certificate, which required a mark of 80 percent or over, the candidate had to answer questions, abstruse in the extreme, which required a knowledge of ancient history, trigonometry, land surveying, navigation, latin, greek, french, and natural science. Of course graduates of British universities were automatically granted a First Class A certificate. At the other extreme, the Third Class B questions were so simple that anyone attempting to pass that examination could hardly fail to do so.

In 1876 the first high school opened in Victoria, and for the next twenty-five years, the requirements for teaching school were no more than a high school diploma and the passing of the departmental exams. Undaunted by lack of training, one-third of the students in Victoria High School in 1880 planned to be teachers. As the salary scale for rural teachers in 1884 was from fifty to eighty dollars a month, high ideals must have been as important as material incentive to these young people.

For many years there were attempts to start a Normal School in British Columbia. At last, in January 1901, after a long wrangle as to whether it should be in Vancouver or Victoria, the Vancouver Normal School was established. The name was borrowed directly from the French system where "l'école normal" was a model for the teacher training schools.

The first location for the Vancouver Normal School was not ideal. Forty-two students were crowded into quarters in the Vancouver High School, and by the end of the first term these numbers had swelled to sixty-one. The principal was William Burns, B.A., a former school inspector, and the faculty consisted of Mr. J.D. Buchanan, "Teacher of Methods," and Mr. D. Blair, "Drawingmaster." In 1909 the Normal School was moved to a large granite building which still stands on the corner of Twelfth and Cambie.

In 1915 a second Normal School opened in Victoria with two teachers, forty-five students, and Dr. D.L. MacLaurin, one of B.C.'s first school inspectors, as principal. The Victoria Normal School drew students from Victoria, Vancouver Island, and the interior of B.C., while the Vancouver Normal School drew its students from Vancouver east to Hope.

The first summer school was held in 1914 and was highly popular, particularly with one-room schoolteachers. These sessions gave rural teachers a much needed relief from isolation and a chance to discuss their common problems. They studied rural science, school gardening, art, music, and household economics. By its second year, summer school enrollment had risen to 217.

In the mid-twenties, a public commission assessed the merits of Normal School training. It found much to criticize, citing inadequately trained and underpaid instructors on the staff of Normal Schools who, in many cases, knew little of the special problems which their students would face on graduation. There was little instruction in the new science of psychology to aid teachers in handling behavior problems, retardation, abuse in the homes, or the inability of some children to speak English. Too often, it was pointed out by the commission, Normal School students were sent out to face these problems with only superficial knowledge of methodology and teaching principles. The report suggested that the Normal School instructors should have to spend several weeks each year in rural areas undergoing the same problems themselves!

The first step towards the self-improvement of teaching standards had been taken as early as the summer of 1873, when a teachers' convention was held at the time of the annual examinations for certification. The next year "Teachers' Institutes" were formed, but the catch was that these were organized by the Department of Education and ruled over by the superintendent. It was not until 1916 that the Teachers' Federation came into being, a body that over the years has become a powerful organization protecting the interests and rights of teachers.

Why did so many young people want to train as teachers during the years when teaching school entailed the acceptance of hardships and very poor remuneration? From the passage of the School Act until the opening of the first Normal School, the average salary of a teacher was $700 a year. Sixty years later, in the early years of the depression, salaries were even lower, rising again to $720 in the latter depression years. Great sacrifices were made to send an aspiring member of a family to Normal School, but often that young person came home triumphantly bearing a diploma, only to write hundreds of job applications and receive not a a single reply.

Perhaps the popularity of teaching as a career was related to the ease of admittance to the profession, and the fact that thirty, forty, or fifty years ago there were few careers open to young people. Young women had

virtually three choices: nursing, teaching, or office work, while men often saw teaching as a stepping-stone to a career in law, medicine, or business. Many of those who began a career in teaching for practical reasons, however, found it to be a true vocation and, despite the hardships, never regretted the decision.

In 1944, the Teachers' Federation took up the cause of the neglected one-room schoolteachers. The brief which they submitted to the provincial government drew attention to the rapid turnover of these schoolteachers due to their dissatisfaction with living conditions, decrepit school buildings, and poor equipment. The federation called the situation "gross discrimination." As a result of this brief, in 1945 the rural teacher's salary was placed in relative equality to that of an urban teacher.

In general, the attitude of the one-room schoolteacher of the past was extremely idealistic. The teaching profession attracted idealists, and certainly Normal School training reinforced this idealism. Great emphasis was placed on "attitude," an attribute which was exalted to the importance of a subject and placed on the student's record. This emphasis on the importance of "attitude" somewhat discouraged the more frank and fearless students of that time from expressing new ideas or criticizing the system. Looking back upon Normal School, some teachers recall feeling rather like young robins opening their mouths for worms, passively accepting the principles fed to them, and going off trustingly into the hinterlands to put them into practice.

Irene Howard vividly describes her year at Vancouver Normal School. Like so many of the students, she was young, unsophisticated, and awed by "the big town." The year was 1943.

"I shared a two-roomed attic flat in a tall, many-roomed frame house at the northwest corner of Broadway and Columbia. The sloping attic ceilings were constraining, as were the no-nonsense rules laid down by our landlady, a Mrs. Miller, who expected the worst, even from two docile innocents like Hazel, my new roommate, and me. Returning from the occasional weekend visit home, we brought back from the farm good supplies of food. When these ran out, we could always buy a nickel's worth of hamburger at the local butcher shop.

"The Normal School was a friendly place, staffed by wise and benevolent old things, watchful and good-humoured, as they seemed to me then, though now I recall that Mildred McManus, B.C. Music Specialist, sharply resisted two students who wanted some jazz for a change at the daily 9 a.m. assemblies instead of classical music. They really did give their concert of jazz recordings—Byron Straight, now a Vancouver consulting actuary, and Peter McDonald, the Ottawa officer now in charge of reviewing Canadian content in broadcasting. And I marvelled at their audacity in standing up not just to Mildred McManus, but to Debussy, Mendelssohn and Chopin as well—I who had listened mostly to the 'cowboy' music of the Dad's Cookie Kids on CJOR and was overwhelmed by flutes and harps in the 'Afternoon of a Faun' as well as by the prospect of having to teach 'Sing a Song of Sixpence' to my classmates under the critical eye of Miss McManus. Yes, she was a bit intimidating with her angular assurance and proper ways, and completely compelling. 'As I was going to Stroabree faih,' she sang. And I followed after, 'Stroabree faih.'

"But art teacher, W.P. Weston, member of the Royal Canadian Academy, who would that year sell one of his paintings to Princess Alice, showed me how to paint a snow scene by dabbing red, blue, and black on the white, and afterwards praised my attempt. Hazel had done my first art assignment for which, in return, I had written her first composition. But Mr. Weston's kind tutelage dispelled my fear of failure and, after that, I did my own art work.

"Grace Bollert, sharp-beaked, bright-eyed, and comfortingly stout, introduced us to Jerry and Jane and the other arcane arts of primary teaching, and had us all come to her house for tea. H.B. MacLean sat us down at our desks, feet flat on the floor, backs erect, and genially showed us how to write with a freely moving and rhythmic arm, not with a handful of cramped fingers. His MacLean Method produced a round, legible hand of perfectly inscrutable innocence. Mr. MacLean was also a magician of repute, and during the year gave a show in which he produced astonishing things out of hats and more astonishing things from the inside of his sleeves.

"We visited the adjoining Model School to observe teachers working with real children. For practice in teaching in rural school, we went to the upgraded classroom run by Zolla Manning. I stood in my turn in front of her class and, afterwards, she said, 'Miss Nelson, perhaps you might wear a bit of lipstick.' I always liked her for that remark. If all I needed was a bit of lipstick . . . !

"Miss Maynard taught Home Economics, beginning with something not too hard—how to make cocoa. She was my teaching supervisor. In my first practicum, I was assigned to a wild grade six class whose teacher kept discipline by stomping his feet. He was a burly two hundred and fifty pounds, and I, scarcely one hundred, could not stomp as hard as he. Two weeks in that class reduced me to tears after which Miss Maynard took me to Purdy's Restaurant for tea and consolation.

"A.R. Lord, the principal, taught school law. He had a fund of stories about the Cariboo, which he loved, and at the end of the year gave a talk on how to cope in a rural school, say at Lac La Hache. For one thing, the single woman teacher living by herself in a teacherage ought to have a watchdog to guard against drunken amorous callers.

"Younger than the others, Ernie Lee, bouncy and energetic, and his blonde wife Marjorie, exercised us in the gym and taught us games and folk dances; Stella Shopland gently presided in the library and read to us, charmingly, picture storybooks like *Wee Gillis* and *The Five Chinese Brothers*.

"This was the second year of the war, but I was not greatly affected, though for the inside track meet I helped write the class skit in which Hitler, Goering, and Goebbels figured. I also wrote the class song and set it to the tune of Yankee Doodle. And at Spencer's, I bought a wool dress in forest green, double-breasted and brass-buttoned. It fit me very well. At the end of the year, I was given a First Class Interim Teaching Certificate and felt myself almost ready to go back to the country to teach in a rural school, perhaps even in Lac La Hache. I was, after all, eighteen years old, and I had lived in town."

In 1956, the Victoria and Vancouver Normal Schools were closed forever. The University of Victoria and the University of British Columbia had both formed faculties of education, and a more sophisticated standard for teacher training prevailed. The student now needed four years of university training to acquire a Bachelor of Education and a teaching certificate. Eighty-two years had passed since those thirteen nervous candidates took the first examination in the Legislative Assembly in Victoria. No longer were isolated one-room schools the training grounds for idealistic but inexperienced young people.

Class in session.

Setting Out

Modern schoolteachers usually set forth to new positions in the comfort of a plane or car, or at the worst, a Greyhound Bus. Most can picture clearly the town or city in which they will live, and if the place proves congenial, hope to settle there. However, in the days when one-room schools were scattered all over the wilder parts of British Columbia, a teacher's expectations were different. To have a job was the main thing. Certainty about the location of the school, and comfort while getting there, were too much to hope for.

Every September, just before Labour Day weekend, a unique phenomenon would occur. Dozens upon dozens of young men and women began to pack their suitcases, trunks, and boxes, stowing away their clothes and every conceivable item which a country schoolteacher might need. Then this horde set forth, travelling by all manner of transport and by unfamiliar routes, to places they had never heard of before. Often these places were not important enough to be shown on the map of British Columbia. Many who began their journey by train or steamship had to transfer to mail stage, wagon, horse and buggy, cable ferry, and even rowboat or horseback to reach their destinations.

Quite a crowd of these young adventurers from the Vancouver-Victoria area boarded the Union Steamship which connected at Squamish with the PGE Railway to the Cariboo and central B.C. The train they caught came to be known as the "teachers' special," and no one could mistake the noisy, chattering throng for anything but teachers. On board, friendships formed at Normal School were renewed; old hands, travelling the route for the second or third time, offered advice to green teachers fresh from school; and a general air of carnival prevailed, with gay young voices calling out, excited laughter, tall tales, and questions by the dozen. Margaret Wilson describes her first trip to the interior:

Travelling to Bunche Lake School, c. 1924.

The 'teacher's special'. Teachers taking the steamer to Squamish to connect with the P.G.E. Railway, August 31, 1933.

"We took the boat to Squamish at nine o'clock in the morning, and we stayed aboard until all the freight was on the train. That night, after dinner in the dining car, all we Cariboo schoolmarms, going north to Buffalo Creek, Riske Creek, and all other places as far north as Prince George, sat on our bunks and yelled back and forth. We called out, 'How do you teach this? How do you teach that?' We had to calm down finally as the conductor was upset. I didn't sleep well that night, the PGE was so bumpy."

The old train coaches of the thirties had their own charm, with their plush upholstery and gilt trimmings. June Day, later a school principal at Williams Lake, remembers her first trip on the "teachers' special":

"The coaches had swinging lamps and a pot-bellied stove in the corner. The washrooms had green baize curtains. If you bent over in there to pull up your stockings, your butt stuck out in the aisle. I remember that every time the train stopped, Indian kids kept jumping on to buy peanuts and candy bars from the conductor. After travelling until nine o'clock that night, we asked the conductor how far we had come from Squamish, and he told us twenty-seven miles."

The train chuffed its way through wild and splendid country with deep canyons and mighty mountains. When night fell and the porter made up the berths, the gay spirit of adventure diminished. Alone in their berths, many of the young people tossed sleeplessly, or peered out the dark windows to see lights from a farmhouse or village—anything to alleviate the feeling of loneliness and unfamiliarity. A teacher bound for a small Cariboo settlement called Ten Mile Lake recalls her sleepless night on board the "teachers' special":

"I was very excited, and all night long on the train I couldn't sleep. The moon was full, a beautiful harvest moon shining across the Fraser at Lillooet. . . ."

Throughout the night, and all the next day, the teachers left the train one by one, disembarking onto tiny station platforms, on their own at last. For June Day, bound for Springhouse in the Cariboo, her first sight of Williams Lake was anything but reassuring:

"When I arrived on the station platform in Williams Lake, there was only the stationmaster; the stagedriver, Harold Mainguy; an unidentified Chinese gentleman; and a drunk cowboy. There was not a soul in sight on the windswept dusty street. I thought I had reached the back of the beyond."

Schoolteachers going up to the Peace River country from the coast followed a more circuitous route. Charles Bruce made this journey in 1938, travelling first by CNR to Edmonton, and then west on the Great Northern Railway to Dawson Creek. The train left on Friday, and he remembers that almost every teacher going to the Peace was on that same train—nearly forty of them.

Teachers who tried driving up to the Peace fared badly in those days. Two who drove in a convertible from Vancouver to Edmonton with comparative ease, found the rest of the trip a nightmare because of the deep mud. Every few miles the car wheels would be completely clogged so that they had to jack the car up, remove the mud, put the wheels back on, and drive a few more miles until they finally reached Fort St. John. Two weeks later, a killing frost cracked the block and that was the end of their precious car.

Those teachers who travelled up the coast, or to the Gulf Islands, often boarded the red and black funneled Union Steamship vessels in Vancouver. They might set forth on the *Camosun*, *Coquitlam*, or the *Chilcotin* if they were headed north to Prince Rupert, or take the *Cardena* or the *Catella* for Bella Coola or River's Inlet. Some boarded the *Cassiar*, the ugly duckling of the fleet, known as the "loggers' special."

Being on board one of these boats was a thrilling experience for most teachers. The boats would glide past steep, wooded shores and up narrow inlets, stopping at small logging camps and out-of-the-way canneries. The main technique for navigating in foggy weather involved the use of the ship's whistle. A short blast was given and the time for an echo carefully counted.

Effie Wenmoth travelled north on the old Union Steamship, the *Venture*, in 1919, bound for Surf Inlet, a company gold-mining town. After calling in at Prince Rupert, the boat stopped at what seemed to Effie simply a "hole in the mountains." She then had to climb up a steep incline and board another small boat which took her across a little lake. For the final stage of the journey, she rode up the mountain on a "dinky" to the mining community where she was to teach.

Edna Davis also travelled up the coast on the same rusty old freight boat, the *Venture*, to O'Brian Bay, near McKenzie Inlet. The trip took three days for they travelled miles and miles, up and down the inlets, delivering freight and mail. There were loggers on board, going back to work after their sprees in town. This was the first time Edna had ever seen a "drunk person," and she found them very polite and respectful. Edna felt she was really living at last for she had a discussion about poetry with one passenger and about religion with another. The crew were especially helpful and the cabins comfortable, with little cold-water washbasins that folded into the wall.

A tiny Indian settlement with the unusual name of Mamalilaculla was the destination of Dora White. It was depression-time and Dora couldn't afford a suitcase so she stowed all her possessions in a huge trunk. This proved embarrassing, for it took a derrick and a congregation of men to load it onto the steamship, *Cardena*, and off-load it again at Alert Bay. By lunch time of the last day on the *Cardena*, Dora was too nervous to eat. The kindly captain showed her the radio masts at Alert Bay, and advised her to wire home if she got too lonely. From Alert Bay, it was a short journey in the Indian agent's small boat to Village Island. Her home for the next four years was to be a float, and her companions, two English missionaries.

Betty Patterson, who taught at Hornby Island in 1921, took the E&N train from Victoria to Nanaimo. She, too, took a big trunk full of books and clothes, but she had a misadventure and left it behind on the train. In those days, a horse-drawn tally-ho took passengers to the wharf where they boarded the CPR boat, the *Charmer*. This small, beautifully-equipped coastal boat catered to overnight passengers. It travelled from Nanaimo to Hornby, back around Denman, up to

Comox and Powell River, and down to Vancouver. Once a week it stopped at Ford's Cove on Hornby Island.

In the mid 1940s, a teacher travelled up the coast on one of the CPR *Princess* boats to Wrangell, Alaska, bound for the remote village of Telegraph Creek. She describes her trip—160 miles up the Stikine River on the twin-screw diesel boat, the *Judith Ann*:

"The day after I arrived in Wrangell, the tide was right and the riverboat, the *Judith Ann*, pulled away from the dock and headed for Telegraph Creek. The Captain, Al Ritchie, made this trip every week from spring break-up to freeze-up with freight and passengers. It was nine miles to the mouth of the Stikine, and another twenty to the B.C. boundary post, and then, wilderness.

"The boat had to labour against a very strong current. I remember how the plates and cups jangled and danced in the galley which was over the engine. Sometimes we seemed to make no headway, and the boat would swing sideways and give a sort of shiver, inching around sand bars. A fellow on the front end of the boat kept sounding with a long pole and calling out the depth. The captain had to be very skillful to read the river as there were snags, and the channel kept changing.

"We passed great glaciers, beautiful towering snowy peaks, and the mouths of rivers whose silt made the old Stikine a sort of tawny brown colour.

"That first night when the boat pulled up on a sand bar near the drift-piled mouth of the Iskut River, I went for a walk, climbing over the huge cottonwood logs. It was almost dark when an arctic tern began diving at my head. I was terrified and pulled my sweater over my head and clambered back to the boat.

"The next day we saw several moose grazing in willow thickets, and a grizzly bear fishing on a bar. We passed the Great Glacier and Choquette Glacier opposite it, and worked our way up the Little Canyon before we stopped for the night.

"The dark forests of spruce and hemlock

Telegraph Creek, 1940's.

Teacher Pauline Romaine taking current-driven cable ferry across Kootenay River to teach at Glade, B.C., 1934.

changed to jackpine and poplar, and on the afternoon of the third day, the boat nosed in to the landing at Ball's Ranch. Across the river you could make out some of the buildings of the ghost town, Glenora, and above them, Glenora Mountain.

"A buckboard with two Tahlton Indians met the boat at Ball's landing, took off the mail, the freight, and me, and clattered up the bank and through the trees. That summer, I cooked at the Diamond B big-game ranch, and in the fall I continued another ten miles up the river to Telegraph Creek and taught school."

Teachers travelling from the Kootenays to other destinations in B.C. usually boarded the train, then switched to one of the huge shallow-draught paddlewheelers, such as the *Bonnington*, which plied the Arrow and Kootenay Lakes. In 1914, however, Verle Moore, who had travelled from Wardner to Nelson by train, boarded a much smaller boat which journeyed down Kootenay Lake, stopping at every ranch where there was a landing. Her destination was Grey Creek, such a tiny place that she had never heard of it. The last stage of her journey was made in an even smaller launch, the captain of which was a rough, taciturn old character. The tired young teacher had had nothing to eat all day long, but dared not complain.

At last, in the darkness, the boat nudged into a little landing—Grey Creek. Verle was bundled off and left to fend for herself. Two men carrying a lantern had come for the mail, so Verle introduced herself as the new teacher, and they took her along a winding, dark road, pitted with holes made by stoneboats. The men called in at several houses along the way, looking for someone to take in the new teacher for the night. Finally they roused someone and Verle, frightened and lonely, found herself in a tiny room, furnished with nothing but a cot and a lumpy mattress filled with hops.

Several years later this same teacher, by now a veteran traveller, decided to move from a school at Silverton on Slocan Lake to a position at Rocky Mountain School near Bridesville in Boundary country. This was fairly easy. Verle put her furniture on the Great Northern Railway at Nelson and started south. From Grand Forks, the train continued along the Kettle Valley route, dropping box-cars loaded with cattle and chickens along the way. From Myncaster, the train climbed up nine miles to Bridesville—the teacher's cat, suitcase, and furniture coming along in the express car—until it reached Rocky Mountain School, perched on a hill like a pyramid, with a log school and a sod-roofed cabin for the teacherage.

One teacher remembers her journey into Bridge River country, not only because it involved riding in the gas car which ran along Seton Lake, but also because of her unusual travelling companions.

"I especially remember setting out to teach at Gold Bridge because I was accompanied by five goldfish. They taught us at Normal School that it was good to have pets in the schoolroom so I purchased these creatures in a pet store in Kelowna and carried them with me in a jar, first by train to Ashcroft, then by stage to Lillooet, and on to Gold Bridge. In those days, you took the gas car from Lillooet to Shalalth, along Seton Lake, a distance of about seventeen miles, and then another stage called Evans Transportation over steep Mission Mountain to Bralorne and Pioneer Mines.

"My goldfish did not stand the journey well. One died by the time I got to Lillooet, and he was removed by the Chinese cook at the hotel with a soup spoon. By the time the stage passed Hat Creek, a second was dead, and I left him in the creek. The fate of my fish was of great interest to my companions on the stage from Shalalth to Gold Bridge, two of whom became progressively drunker as they neared Bralorne.

"I remember the marvelous reflections in Seton Lake, and the dark and looming mountains which overshadowed the defunct mining town of Gold Bridge. I also remember the graceless Gold Bridge Hotel with its thriving beer parlour, and, of course, the fish. The three surviving ones seemed thoroughly depressed on arrival, and were later eaten by the hotel cat. I, myself, did not fare much better in Gold Bridge."

It was by an extremely circuitous route that Marjorie Kenney reached her school at Sheridan Lake in the Cariboo. First, she travelled by boat to Prince Rupert, then on to Terrace, and by CPR train to Prince George. A stage took her to Quesnel where she caught the PGE for Lone Butte, arriving at that desolate station at two in the morning. A man who said he was the postmaster met the train and took Marjorie to an old log hotel. In the morning, the man arrived again and took her by car to Sheridan Lake. Marjorie describes her first impressions:

"There was just one farmhouse in a clearing, and nothing else. It was right in the middle of nowhere. I was shaking. The man could see I was nervous and he said, 'Do you mind being left alone?' Then he said, 'Have you ever done any target practice?' He set up cans and we shot at them for a while, and then he said he had to go. I went into the house. The people had been away all summer haying, but were coming back that night. I lit the fire, turned the chair over, got the kettle boiling, and waited."

Alice Nichols of Victoria also taught at a small Cariboo school which did not seem to be on the map of British Columbia. The name of her school was Buffalo Creek, but the man selling tickets at the bus station insisted that she must mean Mosquito Creek. When at last her obscure destination was located, Alice set out by bus for 100 Mile House. An old man in a Model T Ford met her there and drove her along a back road to Buffalo Creek. It really did exist, and there was the school, surrounded, to her horror, not by buffalo, but by a herd of cows.

To reach back country schools along the Fraser River, teachers rode the mail stage from Ashcroft or Clinton, took a cable-ferry across the Fraser, and travelled by horseback on the west side of the river. The miles of jackpine and sagebrush seemed endless to new teachers. In the early 1930s, Gilbert Yard, an eighteen-year-old Victoria boy, accepted a school at Fraserview. There was no village and no post office at Fraserview, just a few small ranches, and his log cabin school with a sod-roofed lean-to for a teacherage. Getting to this school, high on the bluffs on the west side of the Fraser River, was an adventure:

Fraser View School.

"I received an answer to one application I wrote, but I had no idea where it was, so I went to see the Registrar, Mr. Watson. He was a fantastic character who knew the name of every teacher and every school and every school board in the province. He was very kindly. He pointed it out on the map and told me all I had to do was take a gun and a fishing rod, and I would make out all right. I had a chum who was going to the same area, and the two of us headed off together from Victoria. He went to teach at Big Bar, and I went to teach at Fraserview, seventeen or eighteen miles away.

"In order to get to our schools, we had to go by CPR to Ashcroft, and then by taxi to Clinton. We were met at Clinton by Nels Tait, the secretary of the school board, and he drove us out to the area which was beyond Jesmond on the Fraser River, just above Lillooet.

'City boy adapts.' Gilbert Yard, Fraser View School, 1931.

"I had to cross the river by means of a ferry and go up by saddle horse to the school which was some four miles up from the river on the bluffs. The ferry was one of the old cable ferries, running by means of resistance to the current. They turned the ferry by means of cables to force it across. In the winter, of course, they had to use row boats because the river was almost frozen over. A chap by the name of Jack Eagle ran the ferry. He was quite a colourful character who could take a boat across the river under any conditions. He sat there and waited for anyone who might want to come across the river, and he could see someone coming for miles.

"The road was very narrow and wound down around the cliffs, quite frequently washed out by cloudbursts and rain. I remember the first day coming down it. I would have given ten years of my life to get out and walk, but I didn't want to show lack of courage, so I gritted my teeth. There was hardly room enough for the wheels of the car, and the old Fraser River winding down there below, four or five hundred feet down.

"When we got down to the ferry house, everyone in the district had collected there. They were quite quiet when I was introduced, and they nodded acknowledgment, and then they sat there and looked at me and I looked at them. Finally, one fellow at the back said, 'We've got a flagpole up at the school. We didn't order a flagpole. We wanted a teacher.' I was very tall and thin at the time."

The fall migration of teachers reached its height in the 1930s and 1940s. Although there are still plenty of country schools in British Columbia, there is no parallel today. With modern transportation, most teachers reach their schools quite easily, and although there are teachers who search out the remoter schools, it is no longer a necessity to do so.

Many of today's young teachers take their summer holidays in places like the Himalayas or Tuktoyaktuk, in search of an acceptable level of challenge, discomfort, and culture shock. To have all these benefits, British Columbia's one-room schoolteachers of yesteryear needed only to accept a school in the hinterlands, and set out to get there.

On Living Where You're Put

When it came to picking a place to live, the one-room schoolteacher often had little choice. The school board, or one important trustee, usually made that decision long before a teacher arrived in the district, and very few teachers had the nerve to balk or object during their first year of teaching. The living situation, however, could mean the difference between happiness and downright misery.

In older, more settled farming or ranching country, living conditions were apt to be pleasant for the teacher, but along the railway, and in areas where the country was just opening up, people were often so poor and struggling that there was little community feeling. Jealousy and bickering over the teacher's board money sometimes replaced kindliness and warmth. For the lucky teachers who boarded with hospitable people, it all became a satisfying and happy adventure. For the others, the unlucky ones, it often took an heroic effort to hide their desperation and last out the year.

One of the happiest places any teacher could board was the Mulvahill Ranch at Chezacut. Twenty-five miles along a rough winding road from Redstone is the Mulvahill Meadow—two thousand acres of wild meadow hay surrounded by rolling, jackpine-covered hills, and in the distance, the snow-capped coast range.

The Mulvahill Ranch was originally the old Copeland Place, built around 1906. Here John and Martha Mulvahill settled in 1912, and in the big log house which sprawled comfortably at the edge of the main meadow, three generations of Mulvahills lived.

There wasn't much of a community at Chezacut—four or five families at the most, on scattered ranches. Groceries had to be

Meldrum Creek School and students, 1933.

Ex-teacher Mary Cullum and her former schoolhouse, Meldrum Creek, 1979.

brought in from Williams Lake, and the arrival of the mail, coming in on the stage, was the social event of the week. For sixteen years, Mrs. Mulvahill was the postmistress, so when the roads were snowed in during the winter, people sometimes stayed at the Mulvahills' for supper and overnight on mail day.

Mary Cullum was one of the lucky teachers who boarded at the Mulvahill Ranch for two unforgettably happy years:

"It was a great adventure. I went up to Williams Lake by the PGE and then got a ride with a rancher, Norman Lee, out to Hanceville, then with someone else to Alexis Creek, and then with the school doctor to Chezacut.

"When I arrived, I was welcomed by the Mulvahills and immediately became one of the family. I was like their own daughter. I had never lived on a ranch and it seemed like something out of Zane Grey for right away they said, 'Can you ride? Here's your horse. You'd better learn to ride or you'll have to walk two miles.' So I did learn.

"The ranch house was log. It had been modernized that year with electric light but there was no running water. The meals were so good! For breakfast, you could have porridge with thick cream, and always beefsteak. I had a rancher's breakfast for, you see, the others had been up since five doing chores. There were always potatoes, bacon and eggs, hotcakes, and toast and jam. I always remember when the inspector came because his driver, in the morning, chose hotcakes. He thought it was like a restaurant and you could only choose one thing. When he left, they said, 'My, that man has a poor appetite!' Mrs. Mulvahill had three boys, her husband, a hired man, and myself to cook for.

"There was never time to be lonely. We went to dances all over the country as far as Big Creek—a hundred miles. I didn't get out for Christmas, but spent a lovely family Christmas at the ranch."

In September 1979, forty-six years after her two happy years at the Mulvahill Ranch, Mary Cullum attended the celebration of Martha Mulvahill's ninety-sixth birthday in Williams Lake. She still felt like one of the family.

Unfortunately, the Mulvahill ranch house burned to the ground in March 1978. The fire started under the sod roof and the wooden kitchen roof. There is no fire department in Chezacut, so Randolph Mulvahill, Mary Cullum's former pupil, saved only a few precious relics—the cariboo antlers from the front room, the roll-top desk, several guns, and some Charlie Russell cowboy prints.

With such a healthy and home-like atmosphere, it was easy for a young person to be an enthusiastic teacher, but some boarding places, in direct contrast to the Mulvahill Ranch, were anything but comfortable and happy. Winnie Keevil, who taught at Craigellachie in the 1920s, needed all her natural courage to carry on her school work:

"The place where I boarded was below the level of the ground because of the cold winters. The chickens and pigs made their home in the kitchen. The interior walls were paper and there was one stove to heat the whole area. You could hear the mother say to the boys, 'Take your boots off and go to bed,' and that's all they did. One boy slept on the floor behind the stove and kept it burning. There was a can of coal-oil under each leg of the bed to catch the bedbugs. I washed in cold water and had to break the ice on the jug in the winter. It was pretty cold on the floor when you got out of bed in the morning.

"I sometimes felt upset at the situation. I'd come in and the chickens and pigs were in the house, and the flies swarming around the food, and sometimes I would lie on my bed and weep. It was hard not to feel a sense of revulsion but I had to overcome it. At Normal School, we were taught about what we would have to cope with, and that we must be prepared to live above it. I did face it and I wasn't lonesome because I loved the children."

Orange Valley, in B.C.'s central northland, was the destination of Mildred Haas. In the *Times-Colonist* of August 1981, there is a vivid description of this young girl's experiences, as gleaned by columnist Dorothy Johnstone, from a diary of 1927:

"Shown to her uncivilized, unlined, and uncurtained bedroom, with bare shiplap boards for a floor, the young teacher wondered whether soap and water was non-existent in this country. Along one wall stood an iron bedstead made up with dark grey sheets and blankets under which was a lumpy straw-filled tick. An old tattered curtain in the doorway offered her little privacy.

"Entering the kitchen in the morning, she was asked if she would like her toast wet or dry. Thinking her landlady meant with or without butter, Mildred answered 'wet.'

"Dipping the toast in a dish of water, the landlady served the soggy fare. Mildred looked at it in despair, and then quietly leaving it on the plate, she picked up her lunch and, hungry and homesick, she left for school."

Marjorie Kenney, who taught in the Cariboo, nearly had a similar experience, but she was fortunately allowed to make a choice. There was rivalry for the teacher's twenty-five dollars board money, so Marjorie was taken around to two places by the woman with whom she eventually lived:

"The first house she took me to was dirty and full of flies. The woman was making pickles and she seemed very strange. Then we got in a boat and rowed across the lake to another place where one teacher had stayed. There was no one home so I looked in the windows. They only had one chair and that was for the teacher. Everyone else sat on saddles on the floor. They lived on turnips and moose meat all winter. I guess that girl had a pretty rugged time. The woman I stayed with turned out to be a fantastic cook. There were lots of grouse and ducks, and they'd kill a pig now and then. They did a lot of canning of berries too. Mrs. Levick had to work so hard. She milked eleven cows, split the wood, and grew a big garden."

The general poverty in the back country during depression years meant that most teachers were fed on pretty plain fare. Root crops such as parsnips, turnips, carrots, and potatoes were the usual vegetables, with beef, moose meat, and fish when available.

Kerosene was considered expensive in those days. Millie Morton, who boarded at a ranch near Lac La Hache, mentions that she could not use too much kerosene in the evenings while she was preparing school work, or dire looks would be directed her way. Dressing for a dance by flickering candlelight in a draughty, chilly room discouraged primping in front of a mirror.

Poverty did not necessarily mean that a living situation was unhappy. A town girl who taught in the small farming settlement of Richlands in Monashee country, forty miles from Lumby, recalls with pleasure her year of teaching there. Although people were poor, they had a natural warmth and the countryside was beautiful:

"My father dropped me off at the old Myers Farmhouse, and he hated to leave me there. It seemed very far back in the bush, and the furnishings of the farmhouse were so bare and plain. Everyone was poor in that area in those days, and most people with large families were on relief. The people I stayed with were the grandparents of four of the schoolchildren. Mr. Myers was also the official trustee. I remember him driving up to the school with a buckboard and an old roan horse and sitting at the back of the school to make sure things were going well.

"My bedroom had a small bed with a patchwork quilt, a washstand with a jug and basin, and a small sign over it which said, 'Merry Christmas.' The view from the window was

Myers' home at Richlands near Lumby in 1974, former teacher's boarding home.

over the hay fields to the distant Monashee Mountains. I woke in the morning to the sound of cow bells and roosters crowing.

"Perhaps I suffered from loneliness sometimes, but my strongest memories are of the peace and naturalness of that way of life—the smell of the hay fields, the golden poplars in the fall, the sound of bears crashing off into the bush, the brilliance of stars on snowy winter nights. There was the occasional excitement of visitors or a dance at the Cherryville Hall, but mostly evenings were spent doing school work at the kitchen table. That winter, the news of the Germans marching in to Paris crackled in over the Marconi radio, but the war seemed very remote. I can still see Mrs. Myers reading her Bible by coal-oil lamp before she went to bed.

"I went back to the farmhouse many years later. Although I realized that both Mr. and Mrs. Myers would be gone, I was unprepared to find the farmhouse in ruins—thistles and weeds growing around the windows and the interior filled with grain. After picking my way over the broken floor boards, I stood on the back porch and looked over the hay fields. Someone was driving a tractor out there, and I suddenly felt like an imposter or a ghost from the past. I hastily retreated, got in my car, and drove back to town.

"I have often wondered why so many experiences in cities and towns have faded away while the memories of that first year of teaching in remote farming country have remained clear and strong as if it all happened yesterday."

Although it was most usual for teachers to board with a family or to batch in a teacherage, some teachers lived in hotels or stopping places. Alice Early, Quesnel's first teacher, lived in the second story of the old Oxidental Hotel. Room and board was $20 a month, and dinner was served in style with a Chinese cook and waiter.

Another schoolteacher had the misfortune to stay at the famous Big Teepee Hotel in the roaring gold mining town of Fairview. Headlines in the *Boundary Creek Times* of Friday, October 24, 1902, reported, "Fearful Fire at Fairview. Lady teacher missing and believed to have perished." Miss Smith, a teacher from Armstrong, had a room on the second story of that hotel.

Mary Keenan, who stayed at the 115 Roadhouse on the Cariboo road during the last days of the horsedrawn B.X. stages, gives this picture of life in a Cariboo roadhouse in 1919:

"There was a large dining room and everyone ate at one big long table, family-style. There was always someone from the McKinley family at the table to see that things were passed around.

"All the old roadhouses in those days had what they called the 'ram pasture.' It was the largest bedroom in the place and would have single beds reserved for the stage drivers and freighters, and single men. The going price was 'six bits for supper, bed, and breakfast.' At the time I was here, there was no bar for, during the First War, there was prohibition in Canada. The Federal government could not

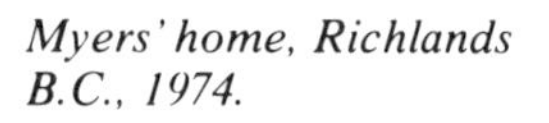

Myers' home, Richlands B.C., 1974.

Left: *Don Smith during teaching days in Peace River.*

Right: *"For the two years that I remained in that community, I did not taste any tame meat. We lived entirely off the land." Don Smith and host family, Peace River, 1936.*

cancel the Hudson Bay's charter, however, and a bunch would get together when they had a gallon and drink until it was done. I never knew of bootlegging at that time.

"The roadhouse, however, was a nice quiet place to stay. They had dances sometimes in the dining room with local music. I played the organ and there were some good fiddle players around the country—Henry Ogden, Tommy Hamilton, Mr. and Mrs. Spencer. We danced the two-step, three-step, four-step, the 'mile a minute' polka, schottisches, and square dances. The fox trot was the modern dance of that time. The dances started about eight o'clock and sometimes went on to seven in the morning. I didn't miss many dances. Schoolteachers got lots of attention!"

As a contrast to life at the 115, we have a teacher's description of accommodation at the Gold Bridge Hotel in the Bridge River country in the early forties:

"Gold Bridge when I taught there was a defunct mining town. There were two hotels, a liquor store, and a house of prostitution down by the river, but no other industry. The teacher was expected to board at the hotel that was not frequented by prostitutes. As it turned out, however, prostitutes might have been preferable to the lone drinkers who stayed on the second story of the hotel where I lived. They made the nights hideous with their groans and cries. There was no lock on my door and so every night I moved the iron bedstead in front of the door."

Of all teachers, the young ones who batched were probably the loneliest. One can imagine the simple supper, prepared from cans and eaten alone, the evening spent preparing lessons by the light of a coal-oil lamp, and the uncompromising silence around the cabin.

A Kelowna businessman in the 1930s went on a fishing trip with two cronies. Returning to their camp at night, the three men passed a cabin and distinctly heard the sound of someone sobbing.

"Listen, what's that? It's someone crying. It's a woman crying!" Impulsively one of the men knocked on the door of the cabin, and abruptly the crying ceased.

"Who's there?" stammered a frightened voice.

"We're friends. Is something wrong?"

At last the young schoolteacher was persuaded to open the door and the three men invited her to their camp for a supper of fried fish. Perhaps she even accepted a small drink, for she cheered up according to the story which was repeated many times over the years.

One young man who taught in the Chilcotin was especially unsuited to the solitude of batching. According to local legend, he became so dispirited that he spent Saturday mornings in bed, shooting at the squirrels that ran along the chinking between the walls and roof of his cabin. Sometimes he visited a sympathetic older teacher, a few miles away, who was a good cook. Once he stayed all weekend and was still there Monday morning when the inspector arrived. To the older teacher's embarrassment, he drove his car quickly back into the bush and bolted into her living quarters to hide under the bed. This less-than-dedicated young man finally departed for Alberta and took up another trade.

It took Charles Bruce of Upper Pine in the Peace River country only one night to be convinced that batching was not for him:

"There was a teacherage there, and I took blankets and everything necessary for batching. The teacherage was a one-room shack in the school grounds, about the size of a granary. It had a bed, a table, and stove, and cupboard, and that's about all. It was a drab affair. To get to the biffy, you had to go away across the school grounds, and you know what it's like in the Peace River in the winter. I didn't like batching! I spent one night there and then started looking for a boarding place for I could see it was going to be a dreary existence."

There are Department of Education questionnaires, filed away in the provincial archives, which were filled out by one-room schoolteachers in the 1920s. The teachers had been asked to describe the areas in which they taught, the conditions of the schools, the character of the people, and their own living conditions. Some of these forms give, in a very few words, stark pictures of hardships endured by schoolteachers in the interior of British Columbia in that era:

"*Soda Creek*—Boarding accommodation is not at all satisfactory. I am at present living in the government jail with borrowed furniture. The people are difficult to get on with."

"*Marten Lake Flag Station*—Living conditions poor. Section foreman's house very noisy. All other residents live from hand to mouth. People seem to have been at loggerheads since last March—uncomfortable for a teacher with a thin skin."

"*Hulatt*—No place to board and no place to batch. This is a new settlement and people are in a struggling position. Present teacher batches with two Swedes in a shack."

"*Stewart River*—There is a great deal of jealousy and quarreling over where the teacher boards. This spirit is carried by the parents towards the teacher, and some of the pupils carry this attitude into class with them making this a very difficult and unpleasant district to live in."

"*Woodcock Flag Station*—Temporarily boarding with the railway section gang. Very unsatisfactory."

"*Palling*—There is no one who cares to board the teacher. I board myself at the back of the school building in a little room attached."

"*Mud River*—It would not be advisable to send an inexperienced teacher here for the community does not have a cooperative spirit or harmony, so it makes the teacher tread most carefully to keep on friendly terms with all."

"*Ewings Landing*—The happiest spot in B.C. for the right person! My fourth year and they still cheer me on. Living conditions pleasant for one fond of summer sports. Winter time—isolated."

This last quotation, which refers to a small school on the west side of Okanagan Lake, provides a cheerful picture and reminds us that there were many teachers who were very happy with their living situations and with the surrounding communities. They were the lucky ones.

By the late twenties, it was apparent that some young people who were leaving sheltered homes and venturing into the lonely life of a one-room school were in need of more help and advice than the occasional visit from the school inspector could give them. In 1928 the government appointed a teacher's welfare officer. Her name was Lottie Bowron.

Miss Bowron was born in Barkerville in 1879, the daughter of well-known pioneer John Bowron, after whom the Bowron Lakes were named. No doubt she inherited from her gold-commissioner father an intrepid character and a capacity for hard work.

Throughout her six-year appointment, Miss Bowron travelled tirelessly all through British Columbia, visiting nearly every one-room school in the province, and bringing solace to lonely teachers with her wisdom and kind common sense. Many teachers living today can recall her visits and her competence in dealing with their difficulties.

A few short records of Miss Bowron's journeys are preserved in the public school reports of 1929 and 1930. In the fall of 1929 she wrote:

"Since April 1st, I visited two hundred rural teachers. I endeavoured to visit as many districts as possible. I journeyed to Kamloops, Cariboo Road, by the C.N.R. to Prince George, from Prince George to Hazelton, to Boundary, and East and West Kootenay, Columbia Valley, Okanagan, Peace River Block, Queen Charlotte Islands, and Bella Coola Valley. In nearly every case where I have been asked to visit, I have later received assurance that conditions have improved. Numbers of teachers have assured me that they feel a sense of security in the fact that there is a woman to whom they may appeal, and who, from time to time, will visit them."

When trouble arose anywhere in the widely scattered school districts of British Columbia, the intrepid Miss Bowron could be counted on to arrive by some means, ready to do battle with the problem. Unfortunately, in 1934, she was dismissed, probably a casualty of a change of government.

The teacher's welfare officer was sorely missed, for the living conditions of British Columbia's rural schoolteachers continued to be quite unpredictable throughout the next few decades. Perhaps it was this very unpredictability which gave teaching in the one-room school the flavour of an adventure.

Teachers' welfare officer Lottie Bowron.

Teaching in the One-Room Schools

Surely it was an impossible task, or possibly the recipe for a nervous breakdown. Take one inexperienced young person; add ten, twenty, or more children of all ages (some of them bigger than the teacher); divide unevenly into six, seven, or eight grades; and put them in a little ill-equipped schoolroom. The teacher must cram arithmetic, spelling, reading, writing, science, nature study, social studies, health, physical education, grammar, music, and drawing into the children's heads, and there will be someone coming to "inspect," to see that it is all done properly.

Lining up for class at Kispiox School.

It is no wonder that the initiation of many young people into the teaching profession was quite painful, especially if they followed the Department of Education courses of study. These thick blue and red manuals outlined in detail lessons for each grade and subject. There were headings and sub-headings, "suggested procedures," "motivations," and "follow-up activities." No doubt the manuals were supposed to be very helpful, but they didn't tell the main trick of the trade—how to simplify in order to survive.

Eileen McKenzie taught in the early one-room school at Castlegar in the Kootenays in 1917. Her first year was a dismaying experience:

"About thirty children arrived on the first day, for it was a large school. I was entirely awed by what I had to do, and I felt very incompetent and worried. There were timetables and lesson plans for all the grades, so many things to do! There were very few books. When you see what children have today, the supplies were so meager. I used a lot of my own books and materials and still I felt I wasn't doing all the things that needed to be done. There is a limit to what anyone can do. Yes, I lost a lot of sleep that year!"

Fortunately Miss McKenzie got through the year and continued teaching in the Kootenays for forty-one years very successfully.

Chris Wright began his teaching career at Darlington in the North Thompson Valley in 1920:

"I think the biggest shock was when I organized the work on the first day and knew that I had to teach grade ones. I had arithmetic questions on the board for all the other five grades and I looked around and found some little Grade One girls in tears.

"It was a hard job because I had to prepare work for six grades, fill the blackboards with

Relaxation break at Richmond's first school. Building doubled as town hall.

seatwork that would co-ordinate with ten and fifteen minute teaching periods, and then mark all that work before I left that day.

"When people talk about how good the one-room schools were, I feel they are talking about the schools where teachers put in ten or twelve hours a day. Some teachers in rural schools could not stand the pressures and they disappeared from teaching very early."

Chris Wright stuck it out and in later years was a sympathetic school inspector.

Teaching that first year was very much a process of trial and error. Most teachers began with huge timetables tacked to the wall, and every fifteen minutes of the day accounted for. By the end of the day, it was usual for the teacher to collapse in despair, about two hours behind schedule. Sooner or later, however, the light dawned for most of them: "Forget the course of study! Combine as many subjects as possible and as many grades as possible, and use common sense." Coming to this conclusion took time, especially if the teacher was conscientious.

Such a case was a teacher called Mary, who taught in a small Cariboo school. About a month after school started, the lady who boarded her sent out a call for help to Dulcie Fosberry, a neighbouring teacher. "I wish you'd talk to Mary. She stays at the school until ten o'clock every night and then comes home and cries herself to sleep. She won't tell me what's wrong."

In response, the practical, more experienced teacher went over to the school the very next Saturday. She remembers it this way:

"I found Mary had missed the whole unit on timetables at Normal School. To make it worse, the wretched previous teacher had burned everything but the text books and the register. There wasn't a clue what they had done in the past, and poor Mary had no idea of combining the subjects and grades. She was completely lost. Hers was a large school with about twenty kids, and of course it was chaos. We spent most of Saturday and Sunday working out timetables for her complicated grades. I don't suppose it was clear sailing after that but at least she would be able to deal with it.

"Mary was a very conscientious person, and I guess she was homesick as well. I imagine a lot of teachers went through absolute hell like that."

By the second year of teaching, the teacher began to develop some confidence. From a very small salary, perhaps enough money had been saved to buy a set of Books of Knowledge or an Encyclopedia. The hectograph duplicator also became an invaluable friend. This contraption consisted of a metal pan filled with jelly-like material. One wrote out a lesson, or drew a map on a long sheet of paper, using a special hectograph pencil with purple ink. This master sheet was then pressed down very carefully on the pad, and by pressing other sheets on the pad, copies could be made—rather messy copies. What a Godsend! Prepared work sheets bought precious time the next day. Most one-room schoolteachers can recall bending over the kitchen table by lamplight, pressing out copies and cursing when they came out smudged. Miraculously the writing on the jelly pad always sank to the bottom by the next night, so they could start all over again.

In addition to the Encyclopedia and the hectograph pad, teachers usually collected their own "bag of tricks"—pictures, ideas for projects, story books, recipes for papier-mâché or modelling clay, instructions for making paper windmills, Hallowe'en masks or Congo huts, Christmas recitations, song books, game books, cut-outs of an Eskimo village, and so on. Sometimes these oddments were enough to fill a small trunk.

There was one other real help for rural teachers. For a good many years it was possible to send to the provincial library at Victoria and receive a box of books on loan. It was a very exciting day when the book box arrived!

Without these extras, equipment was pitiful: a small supply of manila drawing paper, a few sheets of coloured paper, a stingy supply of foolscap, a few thumb tacks, a box of coloured chalk, and, of course, the tattered text books. If the school teacher was unimaginative or a bored old-timer, the school room was apt to look pretty stark, and as art lessons could be conveniently reduced to drawing the regulation cone, cylinder, square, and triangle, creativity could be kept to a minimum.

Tona Heatherington taught at Woodmere in Bulkley Valley. She comments on the paucity of equipment in her school and of how, with a little imagination, she managed quite well:

"Our equipment fitted into one carton—a globe, box of chalk, pointer, strap, drawing paper, plasticene, bottle of ink, bell, and white paste which the children ate. We used old Saturday Evening Posts, English knitting books, and Eaton's and Simpson's catalogues. I can still see a mural about Indians who were basically men from the catalogue in long

Stationers order from one room school at Terrace, 1910

NO CLAIMS ALLOWED UNLESS MADE WITHIN TEN DAYS AFTER RECEIPT OF GOODS

WE CANNOT BE RESPONSIBLE FOR GOODS SENT BY MAIL OR FOR ENCLOSURE

SMITH, DAVIDSON & WRIGHT, LIMITED

WHOLESALE STATIONERS AND PAPER DEALERS

1198 HOMER STREET
VANCOUVER, B. C.

SOLD TO Terrace School Board,
TERRACE,
B. C.

ACCOUNT NO.
TERMS Net 30 dys.
CONVEYANCE G. T. P.

1 only	Imperial Map, North America,	12.60 Eac.)	
1 "	" " South America,	12.60 ")	
1 "	" " Africa,	12.60 ")	
1 "	" " Europe,	12.60 ")	
1 "	" " Canada,	12.60 ")	
1 "	" " British Columbia,	12.60 ")	
	Mounted on individual boards & spring rollers,		
6 only			$ 75.60
2 Doz.	Keystone B.B.Erasers,	2.20 Doz.	4.40
2 Rms.	Cartridge Drawing, 9x12,	1.35 Rm.	2.70
1 Doz.Bxs.	Hygeia Chalk,	9.60 Dz.	9.60
6 Qts.	Peerless B.B. Ink,	.85 Qt.	5.10
2 only	Blackboard Pointers,	.20 eac	.40
1 "	" rulers, 36"	1.00 eac	1.00
1/2 M.	White Blotters, 80", 4x9½,	5.25 M.	2.63
1 Doz.	Weaving Mat Needles,	.55 doz.	.55
1/2 "	Scissors, 820-4½,	3.00 "	1.50
1/2 C	Tapestry Sewing Needles, #19,	.60 C	.30
1/2 Doz.	Spools, Colored thread, cotton,	.45 lot	.45
2 Bxs.	Colored chalk, 3,	1.80 box.	3 .60
	Casing,		.50
			108.33
	Plus 2¼% Sales Tax,		2.44
			$110.77

Paid by cheque No. 13

underwear, with brown paper jackets and pants, all fringed and decorated and topped with headdresses of real bird feathers. Nothing was discarded if it could be used for Valentines, Christmas cards, or paper dolls in the shoe-box peep show. The Depression had taught us how to improvise."

In Tonkawatla School, near Revelstoke, the same situation existed. Agnes Sutherland tells how one little girl improvised brilliantly:

"In those days paints and brushes were expensive. Well, one day I noticed little Annie, daughter of Sem, was not painting but sitting with downcast eyes. I asked her what was wrong, and with big tears rolling down her cheeks, she answered, 'Please Teacher, me loosit paint brosh.' I knew that thirty-five cents was a big item in that family.

"However next painting day Annie was all smiles. She proudly produced a paint brush resembling a miniature witch's broom, a little stick with black bristles tied on the end. She dipped it in her paint and applied it to the paper, but it refused to paint. I asked her where she got the brush, and with trembling lips she replied, 'Barney's horses.' The bristles were a few examples of Barney's mane.

"The next painting lesson, Annie, all hopeful, once more produced a little broom paint brush. She dipped it into the paint and onto the paper with beautiful results. When I asked her where she got the brush, her face lit up like sunshine as she proudly answered, 'Sem Whiskaire.' Her father, with all the love for his eldest daughter, had sacrificed the points of his luxurious moustache to the cause of art."

Taking into account the variations in teachers' styles, the immense and diverse areas over which the schools were scattered, and the passage of forty or fifty years, it is possible to imagine a typical day in a typical one-room school

A hypothetical teacher named Miss Sloan has volunteered to see us through a day in her school. Miss Sloan is twenty years old and in her second year of teaching. She has fifteen pupils in seven grades, and her school is located at Mosquito Creek Flats.

A Day in the Life of Mosquito Creek Flats School

It's nine o'clock on a Monday morning. The Union Jack is flying from the top of the jackpine flagpole and five horses are tied up by the barn.

Although the fire in the drum stove has been lit, and pale sunlight filters through the rather dusty windows, the schoolroom feels chilly to the schoolteacher, Miss Alice Sloan. As for the fifteen children, they stand beside

Classroom, New Denver, 1903.

Who could forget those intrepid adventurers, Dick and Jane?

their desks, not yet settled to the day's routines—closer, in fact, to the world of the horses who shift restlessly and crop the scanty grass by the barn, or to the flock of crows scolding a squirrel in the pines.

Miss Sloan, very neat in a blue serge skirt and a yellow cardigan, writes across the top of the blackboard, just under the border of yellow and orange poplar leaves, "October 23rd, 1933." Under this she writes in a clear hand, "Books are the windows of the mind," this week's wise saying.

The fire begins to crackle cheerily, and with bowed heads, everyone intones together, "Our Father Who art in Heaven, Hallowed be Thy name, Thy Kingdom come, Thy will be done. . . ."

Every morning Miss Sloan reads from the Bible. She always tries to pick the interesting stories, and today the lesson is about "Daniel in the Lion's Den." Of course no one would think of questioning the Bible, except Arthur, who considers asking Miss Sloan if God could stop up the mouth of a grizzly bear.

Miss Sloan is very strict about cleanliness, and that's hard for children who have to walk two or three miles to school or ride horseback through the bush. "How many brushed their teeth this morning? How many have a clean handkerchief? Don't wave it in the air, Mary, you'll spread all the germs. Hands on the desk children. Tom, your nails are filthy!"

After the Health Check comes the Weather Chart. Miss Sloan firmly believes that watching the weather makes children observant. In Science period they have studied what makes clouds form, what causes rain, snow, and hail, and how far the sun's rays travel. Each child takes a turn at marking up the weather for the day. Today's square shows clouds with the sun peering through. Next, Donna sharpens pencils, George stokes the fire, and with some rustling and shuffling around, everyone settles down to do the arithmetic sums Miss Sloan has put on the board . . . all except Grades One and Two who will have a reading lesson.

"Run, sun, fun, gun, bun,—" chant the Grade Ones during their phonics lesson, and then, "Run, Jane, run! Run, Jerry, run! Run, Snow, run! Run, run, run!" reads Mary from the Primer. Miss Sloan stifles a sigh as she hands out the Grade One workbooks and crayons. Privately she is sick to death of Jerry and Jane and their two boring pets. Now the Grade Twos read their story about Mrs. Puddle Duck and begin on the worksheets Miss Sloan has hectographed. "Who does Mrs. Puddle Duck meet on her way to visit Red Hen? What does she have in her basket? . . ."

The reading lessons are interrupted four times: once to give a quick lesson in long division to the Grade Fours who can't seem to get the hang of it; once when Miss Sloan cuts up her lunch apple in eighths and holds up three pieces (Peter can't understand fractions unless he sees them); then again when the fire is burning too brightly. A familiar smell tells that someone's boots are too near the stove. Five seats are moved sideways. Lastly, there is a knock at the door and Tom's father brings in the biggest pumpkin you could imagine! Everyone knows you can't cut a jack o' lantern until Hallowe'en day, but the pumpkin certainly brightens up the room.

Ten-thirty and time for recess. If only all the children would go out in God's pure air and leave Miss Sloan to mark the books in peace and maybe even drink a cup of tea from her thermos. No such luck! As usual, Mary has a bad cold so she and Sue are allowed to play naughts-and-crosses on the board. Then, of course, Angela has to come in too. "Miss Sloan, *please*, can I play the gramophone?"

"Miss Sloan, Gerry's eating his lunch already."

Piercing shrieks come from the school porch. "Miss Sloan, Joe has a dead bat and he's hitting Donna with it."

"A dead bat! Tell Joe to bring me the bat at once! Just what I need for Science lesson tomorrow," cries Miss Sloan.

At ten forty-five, Miss Sloan rings the bell and everyone troops in, anticipating the spelling test. Spelling tests are important. No mistakes at all wins a blue star; five blue stars win a red star; and five red stars, a beautiful big gold star. The spelling chart is right up in front of the room where everyone can see who has the most stars. For a while, Miss Sloan gave stars for conduct, but she quickly realized this was "bad psychology." One of the Grade Twos got a black star and went quite wild. Now stars are only for spelling.

During the spelling test, the Grade Ones have been rolling up little balls of plasticene and putting them in piles by the numbers one to twelve. There seems to be a terrible smell in the schoolroom. Could it be plasticene on the stove? The door is opened and the girls wave their sweaters in the air. Donnie stands in the corner.

The last part of the morning goes quickly. The older grades have silent reading while Miss Sloan tells Grades Three, Four, and Five about the time when most of Canada was covered with ice. She has pictures of strange animals that lived in Canada before the ice came down—woolly mammoths, tigers, tiny little horses, and huge creatures with long necks and little short legs—and she describes a fight between two of these fierce animals. One of the older boys, instead of reading, has been making a plasticene dinosaur under the edge of his desk. He sneaks it onto Miss Sloan's desk.

Lunch time, and lard pails are opened on the school steps where the late autumn sunshine is warm and beautiful. A yellow car goes by on the main road and causes a lot of speculation. Who could it be?

And Sally and Puff and Spot? Reading lessons from We Look and See, *primer used from the 1940's to the 1960's.*

As Miss Sloan goes reluctantly inside to put work on the board, she throws the ball outside. Long drawn-out calls come from both sides of the school: "Anti-i-over, anti-anti-i-over, anti-anti-anti-i-over . . . I hit you! You're on our side . . . you're on our side!"

One o'clock is always story time. Miss Sloan is reading *The Adventures of Dr. Doolittle*, the part where the swallows rescue Dr. Doolittle and the Animals by pulling his boat along with threads at a terrific speed, leaving the pirates far behind! She only reads for twenty minutes and then stops right in the exciting part for the writing lesson.

Miss Sloan tells the children that learning to write is important. If they learn MacLean's Muscular Movement, they will be able to write for hours without getting writer's cramp. Miss Sloan's writing is beautiful, all on the same slant and each letter made exactly as Mr. MacLean says it should be. At the end of the year, Miss Sloan will send samples of everyone's writing to Victoria, and Mr. MacLean himself will judge them and give certificates of proficiency. Every writing period begins with Mr. MacLean's special exercises. Some of these look like coils of fence wire and others like fence posts, or cats and rabbits. The class counts out loud as they write—one, two, three, four, five, six, seven—round and round and round and round and round and stop!

While Miss Sloan teaches the letter D, the little ones practice printing on the board—wavering lines going up and down hill which make the older ones laugh.

The schedule is running late today, so the children do their exercises between the desks instead of outside. "Hips firm! Knees slowly full bend! Arms stretch, arms bend, to touch the floor, down! No Hubert, you've already been to the outhouse twice. Wait till after school."

The older grades have been making maps of Eastern Canada. At two-fifteen, while the Grade Fours help the little ones read, Miss Sloan tells Grades Five, Six, and Seven how Jacques Cartier sailed up the St. Lawrence River and found an Indian village called Hochelaga. The story of Jacques Cartier and the Indian Chief is so exciting that reading is forgotten. Everyone listens, and at afternoon recess, some of the smaller boys scratch out a river in front of the school and pour water down it from the creek. Jacques Cartier's boat is made from a chip of wood.

After recess, something quite unexpected happens! The health nurse visits the Mosquito Creek Flats School for the first time. Right away she notices the mixed-up drinking cups, neither labelled nor hanging on hooks, and the water pail with no cover on it. Worst of all, she looks at the outhouses, and there are some rude words on the walls of the boys', and the supply of lime has run out long ago. Miss Sloan has two bright spots on her cheeks as she promises brightly to do better. The nurse thaws a little and says she will bring lantern slides about nutrition the next time

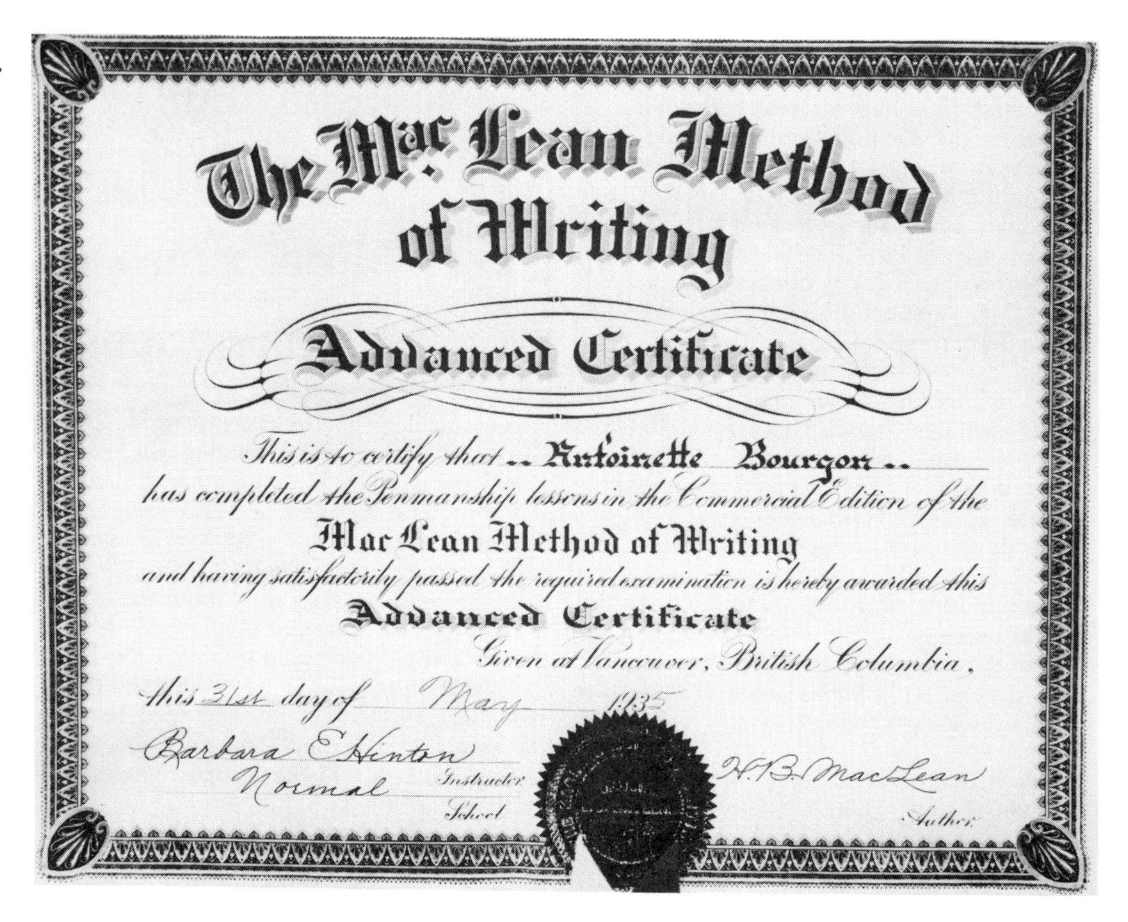
The Mac Lean Method of Writing

Advanced Certificate

This is to certify that .. Antoinette Bourgon ..
has completed the Penmanship lessons in the Commercial Edition of the
Mac Lean Method of Writing
and having satisfactorily passed the required examination is hereby awarded this
Advanced Certificate
Given at Vancouver, British Columbia,
this 31st day of May 1935

Barbara E Hinton Instructor
Normal School

H.B. MacLean Author

Penmanship certificate from the redoubtable Mr. MacLean, 1935.

she comes. She finishes by looking down everyone's throat with the help of little wooden sticks, and talks about the terrible need for a dentist.

Then, very quickly, the health nurse drives away in her small yellow English car, her pretty auburn head up high; back to town and that "other world."

It is a quarter to four when Miss Sloan dismisses the children. She marks the books, and begins to sweep the floor, a little drearily. The nurse didn't notice the paper swallows migrating across the school windows, the collection of seed pods, the rocks all labelled on the window sill, or the children's drawings of spider webs and butterflies—just the mixed-up drinking cups, the untidy cupboards, and the outhouses. The embroidered pattern of her school seems pulled into an ugly dull loop of grey yarn.

Walking home, Miss Sloan fails to notice the golden poplar leaves and the distant purple mountains with the sun behind them. She thinks instead of that other world, the town, where lights shine. After all, she is a girl, not just a "school teacher."

"I see a pig it is so big it cannot run" reads the slightly ungrammatical lesson on this East Sooke School blackboard.

Discipline

Many early British Columbia teachers would have agreed heartily with the stern Old Testament proverb, "Spare the rod and spoil the child." Often these were teachers who had received their own education in British public Schools, who valued obedience and respect from their pupils and were prepared to lay about with a switch or cane to get it.

In those days teachers could devise their own punishment, and they used whatever was available, whether it was a willow switch, a rough hand-hold on the scruff of a youthful neck, or the memorization of long passages of poetry . . . "the sky was the limit," as one old-timer put it.

Strangely enough, the pupils of yesteryear do not seem to harbour resentment against such stern discipline. In fact, if they meet fellow classmates years later, they will often recall with affection and glee, not the kindly soft-hearted teacher who helped children on with their overshoes and mitts, but some old tyrant who used his cane unsparingly.

Reverend E. Fleming of Kelowna attended a one-room school around the turn of the century, and he gives us this picture of such a teacher:

"The new teacher had two dozen children in various grades. Finally he came to the new boy. He pointed to me and said, 'Stand up!' So I stood up.

"'You,' he said, 'say your A.B.C.s.'

"'I don't know my A.B.C.s, sir.'

"'You don't know your A.B.C.s? How do you expect me to teach you anything if you don't know anything? Come up here!' So I came up and wondered why he wanted a

Wild country ways and a wide range of student age were hard challenges to new teachers from the city. These loggers' children from the Knight Inlet area boarded at Minstrel Island under the tutelage of a Mr. Herbertson.

private conversation. As I came closer, he said, 'Hold out your hand.'

"I wondered what he wanted to do with my hand, but I soon found out, as he caned it. It didn't feel very nice.

"Then he said sternly, 'Sit down beside that girl and learn your A.B.C.s.' So I sat down and learned my A.B.C.s. That was a harsh teacher but he had his own ideas of discipline. I don't remember any pranks or sauciness during his regime. I thought it was a bit unjust at the time but it didn't injure me and it gave me ideas. Perhaps some of these ideas about the need for discipline in schools still linger in my head."

But there was another side to discipline in the early days. Although some backwoods teachers disciplined too harshly, there were also very young teachers, with absolutely no training, who could not bring themselves to strap at all, and who could not keep order. Here is Reverend Fleming's picture of such a girl, beyond her depths in the early Benvoulin School in the Okanagan:

"There was one teacher in a fair-sized schoolroom, and about forty-five bodies of humanity, all the way from beginners to great big hobbledehoys who decided a little more schooling wouldn't hurt them during the winter. We were all jammed in one little room with one little girl trying to act as teacher. It was an entirely hopeless embraglio. We plunged in and, to put it frankly, learned nothing. The hubbub, the medley, the whole situation was entirely anti-education. There was a whole succession of short-term teachers at that school."

As early as 1896, a certain Principal Northerby gave a talk at the Teacher's Institute in Victoria. He stated, "Corporal punishment must only be inflicted in the schools as a last resort, as with the great majority of children, kindness and firmness should prevail without resort to force."

Perhaps Mr. Northerby had the right idea. Mr. Hewat, who attended Fairview School in 1910, had a teacher who kept discipline without much use of the strap. He had another method which, to some children, might have been equally painful:

"Mr. Richardson was probably ahead of his time. Our parents thought that his discipline was a little lax, but it wasn't. In place of the strap, he gave us excerpts from Shakespeare to learn by heart, and repeat the next day. My young brother was in the First Reader and he was busy trying to learn the Seven Ages of Man. That is one thing I remember very well although I didn't understand most of it. It was just words, you know, but it gave me a real love for Shakespeare. Years later I'd be working at something and a phrase would come back to me and I'd get the meaning of it then. I still remember my younger brother quoting:

> Then the schoolboy with his satchel
> And his shining morning face
> Creeping like a snail
> Unwillingly to school. . . .

"We had the strap, sure, but it wasn't used very much."

By the 1920s, although some teachers continued to flay about with anything that came to hand, the strap was recognized as the right way to inflict physical punishment, and then, only as a last resort. Sheila Johnson, who taught at Dorr in the East Kootenays in 1929, describes buying her strap before beginning her career as a teacher:

"Of course you know, each teacher bought her own strap, and you always had it in your middle drawer. I think some teachers used to leave it on top of the desk. I bought mine in Victoria. . . I still have it. It's about fourteen or sixteen inches long, with a hole in the end that you can hang it up by. It actually looked like belting.

"Yes, I used it, but it was an extreme case and as I look back on it, I'd never do it again, for it didn't do any good in the instance I'm thinking of."

Rural schoolteachers were a lot like horse trainers. They all worked alone, with no one to guide or influence them, and each developed an individual style of discipline. Over the years, the wisdom of experience sometimes modified a teacher's over-zealous approach.

One young man, during his first month of teaching at a remote school across the Fraser River, was shocked to hear the kind of language which he had never heard in Victoria floating through the school window. Purposefully, he shot out the door and grabbed a startled ten-year-old. The culprit listened with interest to the teacher's views on swearing, but the strapping which the young teacher felt duty-bound to give shocked him. He looked at the teacher with anger in his eyes and said, with some dignity, "I don't like this goddammed school, and I'm not coming back!" whereupon he got on his horse and rode away.

Later the ten-year-old boy proved himself to be a man by his ability to haul wood with a team, and cut it up for the school, just as he had done by swearing, like all the proper men he had known in his short life. The teacher had the good sense to learn from this incident.

Alice Nichols taught at Buffalo Creek in 1939. She felt that a teacher who didn't use the strap lost respect:

"That's the way we thought in those days. You never liked giving the strap and I don't think you ever gave it when you felt it was wrong, but they remembered it well. You had to try to make yourself tough."

Dick Downey, who taught near Pouce Coupé in the Peace River country, believed that empathy with children and consistency in dealing with them are the two most important factors:

"Sometimes discipline problems are due to lack of empathy. Children get the impression sometimes that you're jumping them all the time, and they become resentful.

"One girl said to me, 'Mr. Downey, do you mind moving? You're blocking off the whole board.' I was overweight at the time but I didn't get angry. I saw the funny side of it.

"Sometimes, however, I strapped and yelled when it was called for. I don't believe in strapping in daily taps. It has to be done well. The biggest weakness is unevenness of discipline."

Children who attended one-room schools were not often really hostile or resentful. Misbehavior usually took the form of practical jokes or pranks, and how the teacher reacted was the main thing. Some children definitely earned their punishment, such as the child who stuffed the school inspector's car radiator full of grasshoppers, or the one who was put out of the school during story hour and revenged himself by peeing in the teacher's overshoe. Every springtime brought on schoolyard fights, and certainly there were enough snakes put in teacher's desks to stretch right across British Columbia.

Ilma Beamish, who taught in Ten Mile Lake School north of Quesnel about fifty years ago, remembers picking up the school bell to call the children in after recess, and discovering a bull snake coiled up in the bell. Instead of reacting with girlish terror, which would have caused the boys to chase the snake all over the room, she simply picked it up by the tail and put it out. Thus, she won the respect of her pupils and avoided having to strap anyone.

Another teacher with common sense was faced with the terrible smell of chewing gum on the hot stove one recess. She scraped it off, but replaced it when the children came in, "so everyone could enjoy it together."

By the 1930s Normal School students were being taught the rudiments of psychology, and the revolutionary theories of educators like Thomas Dewey. Teachers of that era had the word "motivation" engraved on their brains. Lessons were now to be so well planned and fascinating that children would forget to be mischievous. Rallying to this philosophy, enthusiastic teachers outdid themselves in thinking up exciting projects. Instead of dull map study, one teacher took his school out in the spring mud where they happily dug and scraped out whole continents, river systems, and mountain ranges. Another took to the hills with the children where, with bows and arrows and Indian costumes, they recreated the history of that area. Of course, this pitch was difficult to keep up. Children eventually longed for a plain old spelling lesson, and teachers ran out of ideas. Taken seriously, the new method was a high price to pay for good discipline.

The creators of these new teaching methods assumed that all children wanted to learn, if motivated. Very little was said about children who could not learn. Hyperactivity was an unknown word, and the blame for a child's behavior was usually placed squarely on the child. In those days, there were no "child specialists" to confer with, and sometimes a young teacher lost perspective and punished unjustly. Such an incident left a painful memory for one teacher:

"I remember trying so hard to teach an eleven-year-old boy the numbers from one to ten. I went over and over them, but he simply would not learn! He would say six for nine, and five for four, and all the while the other thirty-six kids were jumping around in their seats. Finally my hand shot out and I slapped

Part of the answer was to let country kids be country kids as much as possible. Fort building session, Cape Scott, 1900.

him in the face. Big tears rolled down his face, and my own eyes filled with tears. I don't know what the kids thought. I had never heard the word 'retarded' but I knew what I did was unfair."

In many ways, country schoolteachers probably had an easier time with discipline than did city teachers. Rural children did not usually feel such a separation between themselves and adults. They had a share in as much of the work as was possible, and understood its necessity. They also shared in the play, going to dances, picnics, ball games, and to town with their parents. At school, they helped the teacher by bringing in wood and water, and cleaning the building. Sometimes the older pupils acted as teachers for the younger ones when the teacher was busy. The sense of belonging that resulted meant that most children were not resentful of adults.

Most important, of course, was the fact that the schoolteacher's right to discipline was seldom questioned in the era of the one-room school. He or she might never use the strap, but it was always there!

Ironically, it was a single incident in a one-room school which brought about the removal of the strap, the "teacher's last resort," from British Columbia's schools.

On February 14, 1973, the school children of British Columbia received a Valentine. That Valentine was, and still is, controversial despite the fact that it was given by a lady with a passionate belief in the reform of the B.C. School Act, Eileen Dailly, at that time minister of Education in Dave Barrett's cabinet.

Mrs. Dailly recalls the incident which burned into her memory when she was an eighteen-year-old one-room schoolteacher on one of the Gulf Islands, and which was later to convince her to bring the matter of corporal punishment in the schools before the N.D.P. cabinet:

"I don't think any teacher will ever forget their first year of teaching. I think that it has probably left a great effect on most teachers, particularly those who taught in one-room schools. I will give you an incident which happened to me in the first year, and which did have an impact on my future work as a minister.

"Perhaps I should first give you an idea of the situation which I came into.

"At the end of the war, in 1945, I began teaching in a one-room school on Denman Island. There were twenty-six children in the classroom, all grades, one to eight. The ages varied from six years old to one young man of eighteen, so I had a great variety of children to deal with. I had just turned eighteen and was teaching someone who was almost the same age. In those days, there were no regional school boards. One of the local farmers was the chairman of the school board, and if I needed anything, I had to go and ask him.

In some schools the students rivalled the teacher not only in size but age as well. Teacher Ilma Dunn at Ten Mile School, 1932.

"One of the things which had the most influence upon me was my experience with corporal punishment. When I was teaching on Denman Island, I had one little boy about the age of eleven who was exceptionally difficult to handle. I tried everything I had been taught. I tried praise and encouragement to get him to settle down, but nothing worked and eventually I strapped him.

"As the weeks passed, I found that the strapping seemed to have no effect on him whatsoever, and so I decided to go and see what kind of a home he came from, what sort of environment. Perhaps I could get some assistance from his parents, so that we could deal together with the problems this little boy obviously had.

"I will never forget, one very cold fall night, taking my flashlight (at that time there was no power on Denman Island), and finding my way up to this little old house. I had to pass a large dog and go through gates, and finally I knocked at the door.

"A huge logger opened the door. He said to me gruffly, 'What do you want?' I said, 'I've come to talk to you about your son.'

"Immediately he said to me, 'Are you having trouble with him? COME HERE!' He called the boy into the kitchen, and he said, before I could say anything, 'If he's giving you trouble, I'll fix him!' He reached over and pulled an immense thick belt from the wall and he started to beat this child. I tried to intercede and I pleaded with the man to stop, which he eventually did.

"Well, that was a tragic, sad experience, and it made a great impression on me. I realized that this little boy knew nothing but violence. He knew nothing but physical punishment, and here was I, his teacher, doing the same thing to him.

"So that incident was the basis of me doing a lot of thinking about the use of the strap and of its removal from the schools. There was a tremendous amount of controversy that began to swirl around this, but despite the controversy, I was able to stand up in the legislature and announce that the strap would not be used anymore in the schools. Somebody said that it was a Valentine's present to all the school children of B.C."

The Inspector Cometh

The School Inspector! What other person evoked such trepidation in the minds of teachers. Some, with their teaching careers long behind them, still give an involuntary shudder and an apprehensive glance over their shoulders when he is mentioned; others glare defiantly into the past and think of all the fearless and clever rebuttals they could have made to his criticism of their teaching methods. Often, however, the time spent with the inspector is remembered with pleasure. To the isolated teacher, starved for conversation, the visit offered an opportunity for discussion, or perhaps a weekend of hunting and fishing with a friendly male companion.

Usually there was no forewarning as to when the inspector might arrive. Perhaps he would appear when all was in chaos, when just that once the teacher had no lesson plans, or was feeling so miserable with a head cold that a usually sparkling presentation was reduced to a dull monotone. Some first-year teachers suffered nightmares, such as the one in which a tall man, clad in black, loomed through the schoolhouse door and was struck in his stern, lined face with a flying dart. The teacher, meanwhile, clad only in her scanty underwear, tried feebly to retain order in a roomful of pupils gone berserk.

The teacher's inspector myth told of a relentless critic who appeared suddenly and prowled around the classroom, his cruel eyes discovering every flaw and weakness. While the young teacher made pitiful efforts to preserve aplomb and to remember all the teaching methods, the inspector cast a disparaging eye at the timetable, made sinister notations in his black notebook, and departed without an encouraging word, on his way to torture the next victim down the line.

The inspector perhaps cherished his own myth. He might envision himself as a dedicated educator, bringing new knowledge and information from the outside world to the far-flung army of rural teachers; a man eagerly awaited for all the help and advice he would impart; a fair and just critic, evaluating the classroom situation and protecting student and teacher alike.

Somewhere between these two extremes was the average rural school inspector. His was not an easy job. He spent weeks away

No school was too isolated for the inspector to find. Visit to a remote float school on the north coast.

from his home and family, travelling thousands of miles every year over rough and often hazardous roads, and spending many lonely nights in uncomfortable lodgings. With his promotion to inspectorship, he lost the camaraderie of belonging to a group of fellow workers in a city school, for the inspector usually rose from the ranks of public school teachers. His responsibilities were many. All the schools in his large territory were visited at least twice a year, and he must evaluate the teachers by his own observations and not rely on the scuttlebutt that boiled up in the community. Later, when his title was changed to "superintendent," it became part of his duties to attend all school board meetings and to work closely with the elected school board.

The first British Columbia school inspector, John Jessop, in his annual report of 1872, recounts that, "for the purpose of school inspection and visiting sections of the interior where new districts were contemplated, I travelled one thousand two hundred miles by steamer, four hundred and twenty-five miles by canoe, five hundred forty by stage, one thousand two hundred fifty-five by horseback, and one hundred eighty-four by foot, making a total of three thousand six hundred miles during the year. I have also to report eighty-four school visits, an increase of twenty over last year."

From 1872 until 1887 there was one inspector only, and he was also the "Superintendent of Education," whose duties included visiting the ninety-two schools in B.C. at least twice a year, and also visiting and assessing the needs of the communities which requested schools in their areas.

Gradually, as the schools increased, more inspectors were appointed. The ratio of inspectors to schools varied loosely between one inspector for each fifty to ninety schools. In 1937 there were twenty-two inspectors for the 1182 schools then in existence.

Inspector's reports were vital to the rural school teacher. One copy was sent to the teacher, one to the local board, and one was filed with the Department of Education. A poor report would jeopardize a teacher's chances of moving to a better school, or could even be instrumental in the dismissal of the teacher by the local school board. Certainly some of the reports which remained on the teachers' records forever were unfair. Dulcie Fosberry, who taught at Turtle Valley, tells of her experience with an inspector. Having been told at Normal School that the inspector was the teacher's best friend, she asked him some questions about discipline and told him about some problems she was having. "That is something you will have to work out for yourself," he said, crossing out "discipline fair" on his report, and writing "discipline poor." She never asked for his help again.

Herbert Dodd, teaching at Alice Siding in the Kootenays, tells of his first and only bad report. By some stroke of fate, one morning every child in the school was late by half an hour or more. When the inspector arrived, expecting the morning exercises to be well underway, he found confusion and disorder in the classroom, dashed off an extremely uncomplimentary report, and went on his way. The following year he expressed surprise that Mr. Dodd was capably running an excellent school.

One inspector at Cinema, in central B.C., gave a teacher a very poor report. He stepped into the bitterly cold hall which served as a school and found a full-scale dogfight raging in the classroom. Since the children had so far to come to school, and had to go home in the dark, they were permitted to bring their large dogs to school for protection. In the winter, all the dogs came inside the school and were never any trouble . . . until the day of the inspector's visit when they cut loose and staged a noisy snarling fracas to welcome him. The crowning insult occurred when several big dogs turned and growled at the startled man.

Nick Turner taught at Tatlayoko, a remote school in the Chilcotin. He had little warning of the inspector's arrival, but he weathered the storm:

"I hadn't done my lesson plans for the day. It must have been about the middle of the week when, all of a sudden, this enormous red station wagon drove in. I thought 'My God! It's the inspector! What am I going to do?' So I said, 'Hey, kids, here's the superintendent coming to see what we're doing here. We're going to do yesterday's lessons again, so get your books out!' They were really good about it, backing me up one hundred percent. In fact, they were superb! I had done what I thought was a really good lesson on 'The Cremation of Sam McGee,' so we were busy doing this lesson again when he came in. I had an enormous Chesapeake dog who sat on the front porch and he howled all through the lesson, which I thought appropriate. I said, 'Here you have the mood of the poem.' He gave me a fairly good report after that, for the well prepared lesson!"

At Alice Siding in the Kootenays in 1927, John Lukas had some warning of his first inspection. His school was on a hill and he had a view for half a mile towards Creston.

"One morning I saw this person carrying a brief case walking along the road. I always remember my violent activity. The clock had stopped. I had to set and start it, skim off a few flies from the water bucket, get something on the blackboard, bring my timetable up to date, and check the stove. I really moved! I did more work in five minutes than the average secondary teacher does in half a day! I was all set for him when he arrived. That first inspection is quite an experience."

In remote Mamalilaculla, a small Indian settlement on Village Island, Dora White's inspector, Captain Barry, arrived on the float on a cold miserable day to be greeted by a blast from the missionary lady because the teacher's pay had not arrived. Then, just as he entered the school, the stovepipe parted and smoke poured out in suffocating clouds. Captain Barry, thoroughly shaken, said, "Oh dear! I might as well die here as anywhere," and climbed up on an apple box to put the pipe together.

The inspector for South Okanagan, Mr. T.G. Carter, had quite a surprise when he inspected Gertrude Cavenaugh's classroom at Allengrove. As he walked around the room looking at the children's work, the room was suddenly filled with hundreds of little fluttering yellow moths. There were moths on the inspector, the children and their work, and on everything in the room. The woolly bear caterpillars the children had collected in the fall and put up on the shelves in cans had chosen this auspicious occasion to emerge!

Sometimes the local grapevine gave teachers advance notice of the inspector's visit. On Hornby Island in 1921, the inspector came by rowboat from Vancouver Island to Denman, and then rowed over to Hornby. The people on Denman Island phoned to the secretary of the school board on Hornby, who saddled his horse and rode posthaste to the school to warn the teacher. He gave a stern reminder to the children, "Now you kids behave! The inspector is coming to see Betty today. See that she gets a good report!"

In some districts, when winter set in and the snow grew deep, the teacher's sense of security would last until the roads became passable again. On one occasion this backfired. The teacher in a school five or six miles from Pouce Coupé was in the habit of dismissing the class early several times a month and riding in to town. On one such afternoon, she came on a man whose car was stuck in the gumbo mud. "If you have a rope," said the teacher, "I might be able to pull you out." With a rope tied to the saddle horn and the car in low gear, she did pull the car out of the mud. In the course of conversation, she admitted that she was the teacher of a certain

Winter brought snow and cold but kept the inspector away.

If the local grapevine was doing its job, a teacher always had time to get things tip-top for inspection day. Eburne School, c. 1900.

school. "Isn't this school hours?" queried the man. "Oh yes. I just let them go home." "Do you do this often?" "Quite often. The parents don't mind and the kids love it!" "Supposing the inspector comes?" "Oh, that old fossil! He never comes this way!"

The next morning there was a knock on the schoolhouse door. "Well, the old fossil is here!"

Another teacher who failed to recognize the inspector relates the following story:

"Being on the Cariboo Highway, there were many pedlars and many came to the school. One was selling books and I made the mistake of paying with a post-dated cheque. They deducted it from my father's account in New Westminster. He was furious! In October, I saw a car driving up and a gentleman with a briefcase got out. I went to the door and held my foot against it and wouldn't let him in. Finally he said, 'I am A.R. Lord from the Department of Education.' Mr. Lord enjoyed this and told the Normal School students about it."

Not all teachers have uncomfortable memories of inspectors' visits. Many remember the inspector with gratitude and affection. Pauline Hewat, who taught in North Central B.C., recalls Inspector Fraser as "a very good inspector. He would spend any amount of time after school helping and advising you. I think he would have spent until midnight if you had wanted him to. You'd say, 'I'm sorry, I'm keeping you late,' and he'd reply, 'This is my work. Please continue, and if you want me to return tomorrow, I will.'"

Mr. Fraser is still spoken of with affection by many teachers in that district. Apparently he was a very portly man with an impressive expanse of abdomen. He always wore a vest with buttons and it was his habit to hand a child a pointer and instruct him to count these buttons. One teacher remembers how a wicked urge overcame one lively little boy. After completing the count, he gave the admirable frontage a "test probe" with the long pointer.

The inspector at Hulatt in the Peace River country was broadminded and socially aware. Ellwood Rice, the teacher, had never had a drink in his life, and the inspector was a teetotaller, but he advised the young man, "You had better learn to drink a little or you just can't communicate with these people. This is a very heavy drinking country. I'm not suggesting you drink like they do, but if you're a complete teetotaller, I don't think you'll get along with them at all."

Marjorie Kenney arrived at her school at Sheridan Lake one cold winter morning when the snow was deep, and found a man chopping wood in the woodshed. "Your fire was out and I'm just lighting it," said the stranger. It was Mr. McArther, the school inspector.

Consider the whimsical mind and poetic turn of phrase of Mr. H.H. McKenzie, B.A., in his annual report for 1918-19. Deploring the annual turnover of teachers in rural schools, he wrote:

"To these isolated districts, young inexperienced teachers come as members of a sort of migratory species, their movements not quite synchronized with those of Nature's Creatures however, for in soft September days they come and in balmy June they flit away, and there is sadness in their passing, for in these lonely glens the soughing of the wind in the pines, the murmuring of the mountain streams seem to unite in the ancient lament, 'cha till shiune tuille'—'we return no more.'"

Later, in his 1926-27 report, he remarks:

"There is one activity amply provided for in the curriculum that is sadly neglected in our rural schools, and one that I should fain see given recognition, time and attention which it readily deserves, and I refer to music. Growing up in an environment where Nature manifests herself in a thousand harmonious ways, in the music of running brooks, in the melody of full-throated songsters, in the soft cadences among the conifers, in the pibrock of the 'pipers of spring,' why should rural children of all Nature's animate creatures alone be mute?"

Mr. H.B. King, chief inspector of schools in 1940, revealed in his public schools report a dandy plan to enrich the school teacher's noon-hour break. He deplored the fact that, at lunch, "the children stand around the stove or sit on the ground outside the school and 'wolf their food.'" He suggested that the noon lunch-time provide an opportunity to teach the children table manners, and suggested teachers should collect tablecloths, cutlery,

Nanoose Bay School, 1920. Clara Lee (second row, second from left) returned to begin her teaching career here in 1929. School closed next year.

dishes, and a vase of flowers, seat the children properly at a set table, and teach them the "refinements of social living." Mr. King was perhaps too zealous a man to endear himself to the overworked one-room schoolteacher.

"These early inspectors had the power of life and death over all the teachers," said Charles Bruce who, after beginning his career as a one-room schoolteacher, became superintendent of schools in the Kamloops area. In speaking of Mr. A.S. Towell he says, "He wielded his power very humanely, and we all wondered how anyone could handle a job of such magnitude. The inspector in the Peace River territory kept a very fatherly eye on everybody and he used to claim that he ran the biggest matrimonial bureau in the province."

Mr. Pi Campbell, school principal for twenty-four years, and superintendent of schools for fifteen years in many areas of British Columbia, tells something of his life as an inspector:

"In my first posting to the North, I worked out of Fort St. John. It was a terrible business driving up the Alaska Highway in those days. The windshields got banged up and the hub caps fell off, and the headlights dinted in. You enjoyed the road more in winter because the snow filled up the holes. The only problem was that when you drove along your accelerator froze down, and you often just kept going around a corner into a snow bank. We always carried emergency equipment, a sleeping bag, extra gas, an axe, and so on.

"In my experience, I found the moccasin grapevine kept everyone posted as to my arrival time, and I was never able to make surprise visits. I'd arrive at a school and they'd say, 'We expected you yesterday.'

"In the north country, besides the job of District Superintendent, serving the School Board, and having official trusteeship of schools, we had to inspect the Indian school. I had one at Doig River which was north of Fort St. John. You'd park at the side of the road by the river, honk your horn, and wait. An Indian would come over with a canoe and take you across the river.

"At Doig River, there was a chap teaching who had come out from Ireland. I usually made a point of getting to school at half past eight to get the information from the teacher about progress reports and lesson plans so I would not disturb classes. On two occasions, I got to Doig River and sat there; nine o'clock came and no one appeared. Once, after I had passed the time looking at the kiddies books and not seeing much in them but a bit of scribbling, about a quarter after nine the odd child started to arrive. Finally I said, 'Isn't your teacher coming?' They said, 'We think so.' 'Isn't he usually here by nine?' 'Oh, sometimes.' I waited until a quarter to ten, and then I went over to the teacherage. Another fellow answered my knock and I said, 'Is the teacher going to come to school today?' 'Oh, just a minute. I'll go and find out.' I heard him say, 'Do you figure on going to school today?' 'Oh is it that time? No, say I'm sick.'"

Mr. Campbell sums up his feelings about an inspector's life:

"Well, after I got to be an inspector, I wondered why. It was a very lonely job. You lost the relationships that occur when you're on a staff with several others. It's just not there. The fun you had teaching the kids is gone. You become a sort of figure-head... someone the teacher looked forward to, or feared, and then you were gone."

Although the job of inspecting rural schools was lonely, it was certainly important. Whether an inspector was harsh or easy-going, excessively critical or warmly helpful, whether he inspected for a full day's watch or dropped in for a ten minute visit on the run, against his judgements, the little school, the pupils, and teacher were measured. Although there was no typical inspector, each of these travelling mentors is vividly remembered by the rural teachers of British Columbia.

Woodmere School, 1937. Tona Hetherington taught here during the thirties.

The Turning Seasons

When, somewhere over the northern forests of British Columbia, a skein of wild geese flew southward on an age-old pathway, the sound of their honking might be heard far below by a dozen school children and their teacher. The children, watching the "V" form and reform behind the leader, would share with the geese the certain knowledge that harsh and bitter weather was on the way.

The pupils and teacher of a country school felt the changes of the seasons, for they often walked or rode horseback two, three, or four miles to and from school every day.

In the fall, the air would be crisp and smoky. Perhaps a grouse would start up along the path, or a bear crash off into the autumn woods. Poplars turned to a blaze of gold, and rabbits and weasels would change colour too.

When the first snow covered the trail and lay heavily on the branches of the trees, there were tracks of pheasant, marten, coyote, rabbit, squirrel, and deer to observe, as well as

Carling School in winter. Building now forms part of historic display at Three Valley Gap.

the record of skirmishes between an owl and its small prey, or of a larger animal pulled down by coyotes or wolves.

In very cold weather, the older children who had to walk very long distances to school and who were first on the trail, would light fires to warm up the younger ones. Going home after school in the winter darkness, children hurried, but sometimes toes and fingers were nipped.

With the break-up of ice in the spring, streams and creeks overflowed their banks, and there would be improvised bridges or logs to walk. Bears, just out of hibernation with their cubs, were best avoided at this time of year, as the children well knew.

At last catkins and pussy willows showed up along the trail, and children were eager to report the first robin or bluebird, or the wild geese and ducks flying north again.

Summer brought the joy of going barefoot to school, of eating lunch under the trees, and swimming in the creek. There were wild roses, lupines, and violets, and a hundred other wild flowers to pick on the way to school, and the teacher's desk was usually brightened with a bouquet in a fruit jar.

Summer also brought mosquitoes. Some schools were so plagued by mosquitoes that a can of burning coal-oil was used to smoke them out. Also came the doubtful pleasure of the sun shining hot on the school windows, making everyone drowsy by early afternoon.

Country children were forever bringing a jar of squirming tadpoles to school, or perhaps a wasp's nest, still inhabited by a few live wasps. A chipmunk, hiding in someone's pocket, might emerge like comic relief when the lesson dragged a little.

Whatever the location of the country school, the changing seasons were always the main theme of the school year. In those days, children were not distracted by television, transistor radios, movies, cars, and crowds of people, so the weather and the antics of birds and animals were of never-failing interest.

The best teachers were like the children, responding to life first-hand, and happy to drift away from the course of study. Spruce needles, sharp-edged and three-sided, snowflakes under a magnifying glass, beavers in a nearby swamp, or the Big Bear in the northern sky; there was so much to observe and enjoy all through the year.

Verle Moore, who taught at Rocky Mountain School near Bridesville in 1925, could recall, over fifty-five years later, the incredible number of birds around her small school, and the pleasure the children had in observing and drawing them:

"I enjoyed teaching Nature Study the best. One morning a woodpecker came and pecked a hole in the side of the school. The next day, a bluebird found the hole and made a nest right there in the school, and we could see her going in and out.

"Near the school was a tiny fir tree where a red-topped sparrow made her nest.

"Behind the school a pair of robins nested and we could watch the father going to the little creek for mud. Then, farther back was a little spruce with horizontal branches and on one of those branches we saw a tanager, yellow with black wings and a red head. It didn't fly away but let us watch.

"At the top of a hollow stump was a flicker's nest, and then, on the ground on the other side of the school was a junco's nest. They build in a hole in the ground. In another old stump with loose bark there was a chickadee's nest. A pair of mourning doves had made a nest on another stump. They just lay sticks on the top of the stump. She laid two pink eggs. You could see the yolks shining through the shell.

"The most important to us was a grouse. She made her nest beside a stump down at the bottom of a little hill. We could go down and draw her picture while she sat there. Her little husband would be up on the hill. He would ruff his neck and go 'vroom vroom' when we were too near the nest. The first thing the children did in the morning was to go down and see if she was still there. One Monday morning she was gone. All nine babies were hatched and just the egg shells lying there. She had taken her babies into the woods and we never saw her again."

And the flowers too—

"The flowers were like a garden. It was interesting to watch the changes. One day one of the girls found a western lady slipper on a logging road. It is taller than the pink one. The sepals are long and brown and curl a little. They have a beautiful scent. I could find them today, down that little road."

Lesley Newman taught at Chezacut in the Chilcotin country. He describes the country in this way:

"It's absolutely beautiful around there. My first fall I was so impressed with the fall colours. I made a trip to Tatlayoko Lake where the blue of the lake, the dark green pines, and the variety of colours in the fall leaves, with the snow-capped mountains in the background, make it just like a picture! At Chezacut, there are no mountains really, but the area is lovely with forests and open grazing areas, and the fishing is terrific! They flood the hayfields in the spring. The river just overflows and rises up a foot or two. The kids all go out on rafts as the fish come right over the hay fields. They open the barriers when the flood subsides, and reseed.

"The first year I was at that school, one afternoon there was a terrific noise and we went outside. All the trees for about fifty yards on each side of the school were loaded with grouse. For about an hour they were packed all over the trees. And oh, the migration of the geese! You could hear them coming miles away, and they would settle on a swamp not far from the school. The crows, too, occupied a few trees not far from the teacherage. These are the things I'll never forget, the beauty of it and the sounds."

Winnie Keevil, whose mother had come out from England to teach on the prairies and who knew every flower and plant, inherited her mother's love of nature, and passed it on in turn to the children she taught at Craigellachie School near Sicamous:

"I added a dimension which was nature study. I found the children didn't know the names of the trees and flowers. By the time I left, they knew the names of every tree, flower, and plant, and every bird and wild animal. The children brought the things they found and if I was in doubt about a plant, I would send it to the Victoria Museum which was then in the Parliament Buildings. The curator was wonderful. He always sent back a full description and sometimes was grateful if he had not seen all the plants."

Dulcie Fosberry, who taught in the Shuswap area, also encouraged her pupils to love and value their environment:

"The fall fair was a real incentive. I remember there was a competition for the best collection showing bushes and trees of the Shuswap area. That whole spring we worked on it, collecting and mounting all these on three eight-foot-long sheets of building paper and hunting through books for the names of the specimens. The children lettered the names carefully and we got first prize!

"We made baskets, too, with wild willow branches from the woods near a stream, and also from wild honeysuckle and other vines. We cut lengths, cleaned and dried them, and soaked them in the creek till they were pliable. They were really quite nice baskets!"

But there was a wilder side to country children, and although they could become interested in identifying birds and flowers, their approach to Nature was often more basic.

Arthur Peake grew up in the Northeast Kootenays and attended Windermere one-room school. He describes that wilderness country as it was in his boyhood, and the things which absorbed and fascinated him then:

"Youngsters in those days were in canoes or on horseback much of the time, and guns were as common as marbles. Everyone had a gun. There were hunting regulations, I understand, but I was never handicapped by them. Wherever we went, we carried a gun, even to school, and we shot at whatever we liked. I used to get from twenty-five to forty-five cents for a muskrat skin, and fifty to seventy-five cents for a weasel skin, and about three bucks for a mink.

"We had a great variety of animals in that area. If you moved up over the mountains, you could see grizzly, and around the river you would see muskrat, mink, weasel, lynx, badger, and porcupine. You would see their tracks all over the place and rabbits by the dozen. We would head over the hills by horseback. It was ideal surroundings for a boy in those days."

One of Arthur Peake's teachers got a nature lesson from his pupil which he probably remembered the rest of his life:

"One of the teachers had accepted my invitation to skate up the Windermere, about three and a half miles by ice. It was in the dead of winter. The ice was about three or four inches deep and it was so clear that it was hard to distinguish water from ice.

"We had set forth this night to show him the coyotes. They had a runway where they used to cross to the Windermere side and he was very interested in this.

"We set out from the Athalmer end of the lake and went up the east side as it gave better shelter, and if anything was out on the ice, it wouldn't see us against the background. We were coming along beautifully and all of a sudden we were in the water. We hit an air hole.

"We were in winter clothes. I had a sheepskin coat and German socks. Fortunately, we were both good swimmers. I got my hockey stick across the hole and it froze in a few seconds. I climbed out and hauled him out and we shot back to my uncle's place at the foot of the lake. By the time we got there, we were enclosed with armour. I think my teacher thought I had tried to drown him!"

It was only natural for some Normal School graduates to approach teaching in the country with some attitude of superiority. To those brought up in towns and cities, sophisticated and well read in their own eyes, and with perhaps a knowledge of music, art, and science, or at least the latest jazz, sports, and fashion, it would seem that there was little to learn from people who spent their lives in some dull rural backwash far from civilization.

Teacher Don Hogarth (rear) gets a lesson in horsemanship, Big Bar Creek, 1931.

An attitude of superiority could very quickly change to one of fear, and then, astonishingly, to a rapturous discovery of the joys of country life. Dave Hogarth, who taught at Big Bar Creek on the east side of the Fraser River, was a Victoria boy. When the stage finally wound down a series of hairpin bends to the Fraser River, and left him at the Grinder Ranch, he was almost desperate. In his own words, it was "the back of the beyond."

The next week, someone lent him a horse and he went riding. It was a very painful experience. Everything changed, however, for this is how he summed it all up a good many years later:

"My social life was getting to know horses, and I couldn't wait for the weekends.

"I acquired horses very quickly. I got one from the Grinders and it was unbroken and just about starving to death. I don't know what I paid—about ten dollars, I guess. There was just sparse bunch grass and I staked this horse out at the bottom of a gulch, like a greenhorn would. In the night, it went up the side of the gulch and strangled itself. That was my first horse. It was a bit of a shock alright!

"Anyhow, I got another horse from Henry Grinder and finally the word got out that there was a greenhorn who would buy horses. I got a really good horse from the Murdochs across the river, and the other ones came and went by trading. Horse trading was a way of life in that area. That was my social life.

"The first year when I went home, I knew there was no way I was going to stay out and leave behind the eight horses I had running at High Bar Mountain.

"We were just boys really, and malleable. We took pleasure in the same things the kids did. It was a romantic experience and the horses were a big part of it, and that one year was the point of no return."

Riding horseback across the sagebrush flats above the Fraser River, Dave Hogarth forgot all about his life in the city. He was totally immersed in a world that was natural, the world of turning seasons. Perhaps this explains why teaching school in a rural area could be the deepest experience of a lifetime.

Days that were Special

Country schools marked every festival of the year. Thanksgiving, Hallowe'en, Valentine's Day, and Easter could all be celebrated, as well as Christmas and May 24th. Even a school where there was scarcely a drop of Irish blood might be decorated with pigs and shamrocks on St. Patrick's Day.

All these simple celebrations gave colour and form to the year. Too soon many children in isolated areas learned from their parents to look on life as a struggle for existence. The teacher, by helping them to celebrate the changing year, stirred their imaginations, and perhaps the children did learn something at a deeper level from the symbols.

At Thanksgiving there was usually a special blackboard border of fruit, vegetables, and autumn leaves, or colourful turkeys. These borders could be made with stencils—paper patterns with designs pricked into them. When the teacher held the pattern against the blackboard and hit it with a blackboard brush full of white chalk, the design showed up. The designs were then coloured with fancy chalk, which came in a box packed with sawdust and was too precious to be used for every day things.

Most teachers told the children that they should all be very thankful for the harvest, and some went on to tell the story of the Pilgrim Fathers who were fed by the Red Indians. Small children understood about the harvest, but some may have wondered if there were Pilgrim Mothers too.

A few weeks later would be the Hallowe'en party. At recess or noon hour of that special day, the oldest boys, receiving plenty of advice from the whole school, would cut the face on the pumpkin with a jackknife. After lunch, the children waited impatiently for the moment when the teacher would light the candle in the pumpkin, for that meant the party was going to begin. With its burnt pumpkin smell, the jack o'lantern grinned from the darkest corner of the room, while black cats prowled along the windows and bats hung from the ceiling.

Hallowe'en games were usually the simple old-fashioned kind. Desks were pushed back and, kneeling around a washtub, hands behind their backs, the children tried to bite the floating apples. Afterwards, long peelings cut from the apples could be thrown over the children's shoulders, falling, hopefully, in the shape of a sweetheart's initial. More often than not, the peelings would hurtle erratically across the room, breaking into pieces, or falling prophetically into the wastebasket.

If the teacher had been to town, the children might feast on black and orange jelly beans while she told a ghost story. Someone must

May Day celebrations, Francois Lake, 1951.

Halloween party, Irvines Landing.

howl at the right place in the story, another moan, and a witch cackle. The unaccustomed bedlam was wonderful, but often the ghosts became very real to the smaller children so that when it was time to go home, a steer looming up on the road seemed terrifying.

Some schools celebrated with a bonfire, and real fireworks set off by one of the fathers. One teacher gave sparkle sticks as prizes so that the children went down the darkening road in a burst of glory, turning and twisting and disappearing in the frosty twilight, like comets.

Valentine's Day was introduced by a story. The teacher told the children about a good man called St. Valentine who lived a long time ago. Because he was so kind to poor people, we send messages of love on his birthday. The shaky connection between this story and the broken hearts and arrows on the Valentine card was never explained by the teacher.

The Valentine Box, festooned with hearts and crepe paper ribbons, stayed on the teacher's desk for a week. During that week, the children were busy making Valentines. The girls poked them into the slit on the top of the Box by the handful, but some of the boys didn't want to be seen putting anything in the Box. Those children who were lucky enough to have store-bought Valentines, with real lace and fold-outs, usually sent them to the teacher.

As the day drew closer, the Box seemed to grow larger. All through arithmetic, spelling, and reading lessons, it sat on the teacher's desk, full of mysterious secrets.

At last, at two o'clock on St. Valentine's Day, the teacher would borrow a knife from one of the boys. The room became very quiet as the Box was slit open. The oldest boy was postman and the oldest girl, in a headdress of hearts, walked importantly around the room delivering the valentines. After awhile, it was easy to see how many messages of love the box held for some children and how few for others. The children with the least valentines usually hid their hurt feelings by making silly jokes and eating more than their share of candy. It is doubtful if any teacher ever explained the difference between love and popularity.

The day after Valentine's Day always seemed very peaceful. The Box was gone and everything was back to normal.

At Easter, the room was decorated again, but this time with symbols of spring. Some teachers read the Easter story from the Bible while others avoided this emotional subject and concentrated on an Easter egg hunt in the woods around the school, with hard-boiled eggs, which the children coloured, and candy eggs from town.

Children also made Easter cards for their parents. One teacher took the children, on a Friday afternoon, to a nearby slough to pick pussy willows. There were red-winged blackbirds, swaying and calling in the rushes, and tadpoles along the edge of the slough. Back at the school, everyone, even the older children, pasted the pussy willows onto cards so that they looked like Easter rabbits. The pleasure of this for the teacher was that for an hour there was no sound but the snipping of scissors, and the sniffling of several children with spring colds. Under each rabbit was printed, "Happy Easter, Mother and Dad." Of course, the rabbits would be lucky if they kept their fur until Easter morning. Most teachers learned to distrust library paste.

Christmas was the greatest celebration of the school year, not only for the children but for the whole of a rural community. Next to Christmas in importance was the School Picnic, usually held on May 24th. There follow descriptions of these two events in a district called Willow Creek.

Christmas Program – Willow Creek School 1934

1. Welcome Poem—Douglas Roberts
2. "Come All Ye Faithful," "The First Noel" —Sung by the whole school
3. Christmas Acrostic—The whole school
4. Recitation, "My New Doll"—
Mary Dempster
5. "Hiram's Courtship"—
A comical play by the grade eight pupils
6. Drill—"Ten Little Indians"
Song—"Oh Christmas Tree, Oh Christmas Tree"—Junior grades
7. "The Silver Sage Cowboys"
and the Ritter Boys
8. "Over the Waves,"<br>"Life in the Finland Woods"—
accordion solos by Mr. J. Nordstrom
9. Patriotic Flag Drill—
"Canada, our Native Land"—
Grades 4 to 8
10. "Blueberry Hill,"<br>"My Daddy is Only a Picture"—
Duets by Betty and June Dempster
11. "The Christmas Story"—
A Nativity Play by the whole school

All sing—"Here Comes Santa Claus"
—"Jingle Bells"

The Christmas Concert – Highlight of the Year

Longed for by all the school children, the Christmas concert is almost too exciting and happy an event to bear! For the teacher, however, it is different. Almost before the Hallowe'en party is over, she begins to feel twinges of anxiety. The Christmas concert, she realizes suddenly, is only seven weeks away, and she has absolutely no inspiration. Her sleep becomes troubled and she finds it hard to concentrate on the usual school routine; the slowly approaching Christmas concert has assumed the proportions of a time-bomb.

All rural school concerts were really variations on a theme, but it was the variations that caused the desperation. How to put on a really interesting concert with only a few pupils and not even a piano to practice with? By November she wails to herself, "Whatever shall I do that is different this year? Everyone for miles around will be there, even the teachers from Pine Grove and West Fork, and I'm sure my concert will be a flop!" Night after night at the kitchen table she thumbs through catalogues of plays, recitations, carols, drills, school readers, until, slowly, this year's concert begins to take a vague shape in her mind.

Overnight the crisis is over. Now frantically creative, the teacher makes angel wings from old net curtains, a horse's head from the map of Africa, headdresses from turkey feathers, dwarf faces from stockings, and a beard for Joseph from tree moss. It is a great relief when some mothers offer to make the costumes for the "Canada Flag Drill" from flour sacks.

Then the practice begins, wearing a track in the brains of the children which time can never erase. . . . "Oh Christmas Tree, Oh

Christmas Tree," "Old Faithful," "We Rode the Range Together," "H is for the Holly Wreath so Gay," "We Wish You a Merry Christmas," "Oh Come All Ye Faithful," "Hip Hip Hooray for Canada," "Noel, Noel, Noel". . . . There is no piano in the school, so teacher does her best to keep everyone together with a tuning fork. "At least we'll all start out together, and everything will sound fine in the hall if Mr. Taylor plays the piano loud enough."

Utter exhaustion is reached by the time the mothers have helped the teacher sew fifty green-and-red net bags, one for each child in a radius of ten miles, even the babies. Each bag is filled with candy, nuts, and a bright orange. All the little gifts which were ordered from Eaton's are wrapped and ready to go in Santa's pack. The bachelors contributed especially generously this year.

The night of the Christmas concert arrives, like all truly great events, with almost dream-like immediacy. Soft snow is falling as horses, cars, and trucks pull up to the log community hall. The gas lamps are lit, and someone is stoking the big drum stove. There are fragrant fir boughs around the stage at one end of the hall, and above the sagging sheet curtains, tinsel letters say, "Merry Christmas to All." Most beautiful and longed for sight is the Christmas Tree. Reaching almost to the ceiling, decorated with paper chains, tinsel, and balloons, and hung about with the green and red bags of candy, it stands shining proudly by the stage. The whole hall smells of pine boughs and oranges.

Soon the hall begins to fill with a buzzing expectancy as families greet each other, stamp off the snow, and admire the tree. The school children, scrubbed and shining, are unbearably happy and excited, but they also feel a little frightened, as they rush behind stage to find teacher. Some little ones run up to the tree and have to be pulled back before the balloons are broken. As for the teacher, she looks quite calm and especially pretty in a red dress. It is too late to worry; she has done her best. Besides, it will all be over in a few hours!

How reassuring it is to see old Mr. Taylor at the piano, rearranging the music, and the older boys, so responsible, looking after the curtains. Santa Claus is another matter. He has been into the home-brew and, dressed too soon in his costume, he tends to slide down the wall back of the stage. One of the fathers takes him out in the cold air behind the stage to sober up.

At eight o'clock sharp, the curtains swing, bulge, and part as Douglas Roberts is almost pushed out in front. He recites a "Welcome Poem" in a clear, strong voice. Douglas says afterwards that his knees were knocking, but no one would ever guess it.

Next the whole school lines up, big ones on the outside, little ones in the middle, and sings "Oh Come All Ye Faithful," and "The First Noel." The concert is off to a good start.

After a Christmas acrostic, the smallest child has a piece to say, practiced for weeks at school and coached at home by her elder sister. It is only four lines long:

> My voice seems awfully big,
> And I seem awfully small,
> I came up here to speak a piece
> And show you MY NEW DOLL!

She marches to centre stage, clutching a doll, and very conscious of the new pink ribbon in her hair. Alas, she remembers only the first two lines and bursts into tears. It is early in life to know such feelings of disgrace and failure. Teacher mops up the tears distractedly, for her mind is on the next play and the headdresses for the "Ten Little Indians."

The play the four oldest pupils put on, and which the teacher sent for through French's catalogue ("suitable for young teen agers, a real audience-pleaser), is an instant hit. It is called "Hiram's Courtship." People do laugh, but mostly because Hiram reminds them of a local bachelor with a similar name. The hilarity carries on through the next skit, but it is *not* the "ten little Indians'" fault! Somehow the wire holding up the blanket breaks, leaving six little Indians crouched down and four up. It's no use going on; Mr. Wilson falters at the piano, and the ten little Indians bolt, while the audience laughs heartily. The ten recoup themselves by marching back on stage without their headdresses, to sing "Oh Christmas Tree."

The next part of the program is the favourite of all the boys . . . "The Silver Sage Cowboys." The camp-fire, made from red crepe paper and logs, with a lantern behind, looks almost real in the dark, especially when Ronnie Larson howls like a coyote off-stage. There is a horse in the play. It is made from painted maps and a blanket, and has two boys inside it—the front end and the back end. The teacher had a hard time getting someone to be the back end. The boys in the upper grades sit around the fire dressed as cowboys and sing three songs: "You Are My Sunshine," "Red River Valley," and "Tumblin' Tumbleweed." The Ritter boys chord for them. The Ritter boys are older and don't go to school any more. They have mail order guitars and know all the latest western songs because their father bought a Marconi radio. It is nice of them to chord, but then they get a chance to sing in their satin shirts and cowboy hats. Everyone really applauds when the Ritters play their theme-song, "Silver on the Sage Tonight," but then, to teacher's horror, they play a song that's not even on the program. The words are terrible for a school concert, "I'm in the Jail House Now, I'm in the Jail House Now—Yodel-a-ee-ooo!" To make matters worse, the horse is frisky, backs up too far, and falls blindly over the camp-fire and off the stage, right in the middle of "Tumblin' Tumbleweed" (an accident which will be gleefully recalled for the next thirty years).

Things get back to normal when a favourite older bachelor comes up with his accordion and plays "Over the Waves" and "Life in the Finland Woods." This gives the teacher a chance to help children struggle into their costumes for "The Canada Flag Drill."

"Canada, our Native Land" is a patriotic flag drill. The ten provinces are dressed in costumes made by their mothers from flour sacks, dyed red and blue. They have white banners across their chests, telling which province each one represents, and colourful maple leaves on their backs. Mr. Taylor plays "The Maple Leaf Forever" as the provinces march in formation and wave their flags. At the end, "Canada" herself comes in, crowned with maple leaves and carrying the Union Jack. Then, with their flags held up in a circle, the Provinces and Canada sing a song which begins:

Hip, hip, hooray for our Native Canada,
The Queen of the Summer,
and the Lady of the Snow . . .

The teacher and the children are all very relieved and proud when the flag drill is over without a single mishap.

Now the fifteen-year-old twins, Betty and Jean Dempster, come out in front of the curtain and sing, in harmony, "I Found My Thrill on Blueberry Hill," and a sad song called "My Daddy is Only a Picture." Their parents are proud when someone whispers loudly, "They're good enough to be on the radio!"

And now, at last, comes the most important part of the concert, the "Christmas Pageant." One final mishap almost leads to tragedy. A careless angel holds her candle too close to Joseph's beard as they line up back stage. Teacher quickly wrenches off the beard, only to drop it in a manger of straw. With great presence of mind she stifles the blaze with a blanket, and seconds later, while teacher trembles and shakes, a blissfully ignorant audience watches Mary and clean-shaven Joseph gaze raptly down at the cradle. Baby-doll Jesus smiles back with innocent eyes. The angels stand with outstretched wings, holding courageously still through the approach of all the Wise Men in dressing gowns, and Shepherds in potato sacks, while the children sing "While Shepherds Watched Their Flocks by Night" and "We Three Kings."

Then, the last and most beautiful carol of all! Everyone sings as the angels' wavering candles shine on the children's faces, and on Mary and Joseph kneeling by the cradle.

Silent Night, Holy Night,
All is Calm, All is Bright,
Round yon Virgin Mother and Child,
Holy Infant so Tender and Mild,
Sleep in Heavenly Peace,
Sleep in Heavenly Peace.

The curtains slowly close, and for a moment the hall is still; the beloved old song touches the hearts of young and old.

Then up jumps one of the fathers to report that Santa Claus is flying over Fletcher's Pond. One of the reindeers has a lame leg, so Santa may be just a little late. This is Mr. Taylor's cue to play "Jingle Bells" and "Here Comes Santa Claus," until at last, with a ring of bells, Santa comes chiming and ho-hoing and reeling in the side door of the hall. The scotch tape was not renewed on his whiskers this year and they droop to one side. Nevertheless he is a good Santa, sweating profusely behind his mask, and jovially asking each child the same question, "Have you been a good girl? . . . Have you been a good boy?" Even the frightened babies get a net bag with an orange and candy, and each child, young and old, clutches a gift, wrapped in bright paper and ribbons and taken from Santa's pack.

Now the centre of excitement begins to shift. Stout ladies are busy heating a big boiler on the cook stove in the kitchen. Benches are pulled against the wall, and the fiddler, who disappeared back stage to fortify himself, is unwrapping his violin and putting rosen on his bow. Pandemonium reigns back stage, as poor teacher tries to sort out each child's belongings amidst a discouraging welter of angel's wings, hay, cowboy costumes, the crepe paper bonfire, the defunct horse, and all the tinsel acrostic letters of "Merry Christmas."

The Christmas dance continues on into the night, as snow silently covers the cars, horses, and pick-up trucks, and sweat trickles down the faces of the fiddler and the accordion player. Babies, snuggled on coats under the benches, wake and cry, and sleep again; larger children, too tired to run any more, slump at last and sleep wherever they can; but the teenagers two-step and waltz and polka and docey-do as if they wish the Christmas dance would never end. The teacher dances too. Giddy and flushed from exhaustion and relief, she drops her reserve, and everyone watches slyly to see which partner she favours. And after the salmon and egg sandwiches, and the cups of coffee and creamcake, and one more square, and "Home Sweet Home," and "Good Night Ladies," the Christmas dance winds to a close.

The first to leave are surprised, for the snow has stopped falling, and the air is crisp and clear. Fence posts and trees are sparkling. Soon the beautiful silent night is broken by the crunching of snow, the sound of cars being cranked, of harness and bells, and of a sleepy child crying. Neighbours call out "Merry Christmas! Merry Christmas!" The Christmas concert is over for one more year.

Sports Day, Marguerite School, 1931. L to R: Dorothy Williams, Lois Bell, Elsie Randall, Mary Bell, June Macalister, Irene Macalister, Frances Macalister, Edward Williams, Bob Macalister, Ralph Williams, Roy Williams.

The School Picnic

One of the great social events of the rural school year was the school picnic. This was true all over Canada, even in the far north, until fairly recent times. The occasion provided an opportunity for families to leave all their chores behind, and relax with their neighbours in the sunshine. It was a celebration of summer.

The games and races, the tug-of-war, and the ball game, were intended simply for fun and sociability, so the rural school picnic bore little resemblance to the modern school "Sports Day." No one ever practiced *seriously* for a school picnic!

As soon as the picnic date was decided, the teacher made a long and rather strange list of things she would need. Perhaps the list would look something like this:

Things to collect for the picnic

nine potato sacks
seven silk stockings
twelve potatoes
six spoons
twelve balloons
ten threaded needles
ball of string
rope for the tug-of-war (Ask Joe W.)
bucket and dipper
two balls and bats
cap gun and caps (ask Jimmie)
pins

From Town

3 doz. lemons
ten lbs. sugar
1 lb. coffee
75 ice cream cones
2 yds. each blue, red, white ribbon

The sound of rain falling on the roof the night before the school picnic was good reason for worry and lack of sleep. In memory, however, the sun always seemed to shine brightly on that special morning. Birds sang at the picnic spot, and wild flowers bloomed under the trees where some little creek sparkled and shimmered over pebbles and stones, and then ran deep and dark under the alder trees.

At nine o'clock on a morning in late May or early June, children and their parents, interested neighbours, and the teacher, met in front of the little school. All the collected paraphernalia: food brought by the mothers, materials for games, planks for the table, the precious freezers of ice-cream, and a sack of ice . . . all this was loaded onto someone's truck or car or wagon. Then everyone piled gaily in and the bumpy ride to the picnic spot began, usually over rutted, little-used roads.

An hour later, the picnic began to take shape. First the children were unloaded, and before they could be warned or instructed, they disappeared in all directions, whooping joyfully, exploring (in their best clothes) the woods and hills, and jumping across the creek on stepping stones. Some got soaking wet in the first half hour while trying to catch brook

The Great Easter Egg Race, Ootsa Lake, 1944.

trout with their hands, others tangled with a bee's nest and came screaming back for sympathy.

Meanwhile, some of the men looked the ground over and decided on the best stretch of grass for the races. One paced out thirty, fifty, and sixty yards, while another marked the start and finish lines. The ladies directed their husbands to make a table of planks under the trees, fill the pails from the creek, and collect firewood.

Finally, after a struggle, the children were rounded up, and the foot races began. The teacher was usually happy to hand over her list of events to two or three of the fathers, for she had the task of sorting out and lining up the excited children for each race: first, the thirty-yard dash for seven and under; the fifty-yard dash for twelve-year-old boys and under; the fifty-yard dash for girls; the sixty-yard dash for sixteen-year-olds and under, and so on.

The bachelors' and the ladies' races were the cause of great hilarity. Some protesting ladies were offered a handicap, being overweight and short of breath.

The sack race was a favourite of the smaller children. Six or seven would begin to hop manfully down the field, swathed in potato sacks that would not stay up, falling only to rise again, hopping with even greater determination when all hope was gone. There would be much cheering from the sidelines. "Come on, Herby!" "Hurry up, Johnny!" "Jump, Mary, jump, jump!" The hopeless losers trailed their sacks back to the starting line, wishing to try again.

Next, the three-legged race! In this race, partners, willing and unwilling, were tied together by the ankle with the teacher's silk stockings. They must cooperate or fall together. Some unlucky, independent types could not adjust to this close partnership, so both fell and, despite their struggles, could not rise again. Cross words sometimes resulted as cheers rang out for the winners—usually a long-legged pair with the foresight to practice before the race began.

The potato race posed a great temptation to cheat, just a *little* bit. Teacher put four piles of even-sized potatoes at the end of the field and relay teams were chosen. The cap-gun was fired and each team member tore down the field, spoon in hand, to pick up a potato. Some overshot the mark in their excitement. Others, carried away by the urging

Lining up for the sack race.

of their team and despite the teacher's stern warning, used their thumbs to hold the potatoes on the spoons.

The wheelbarrow race was great sport for those who watched, but very hard on the wheelbarrows! For some reason, an unfortunate smaller child was usually chosen to be the wheelbarrow, while an older, more aggressive child grasped his ankles and propelled him along the track. He hoped to win by pushing with all his might. Usually the "wheelbarrow" collapsed under the strain and was then good-naturedly blamed for his failure to stay upright. Wheelbarrows should have been chosen for their strong arms.

By the time the needle-and-thread race was over, and the balloons had all been batted to the finish line, most of the children were pinned with several ribbons, perhaps a blue, two reds, and a white. In affluent times, nickels and dimes were the rewards, or the promise of an extra ice-cream cone. Some children had no prizes at all, but this was never counted a tragedy or a disgrace.

The tug-of-war was more serious business. Two men chose their sides, paying special attention to weight. Even the stout ladies who could not race well were now in demand, but small children were not chosen, as they could be trampled on during the struggle. Two lines were drawn in the earth, about ten feet apart. The trick was to pull the enemy team across the line, into your territory. The centre point of a long strong rope was marked, and the teams took their places along the rope as directed by the team captain, with a strong "anchor man" at the end. Already the team members would feel an intense loyalty. The captains, not touching the rope, stood beside their teams, calling and exhorting them to pull in unison. "Pull!pull!pull!" Slowly one team began to make headway. The rope moved inch by inch . . . and then there was a deadlock. Faces were flushed, hair awry, and teeth clenched as the rope moved in the opposite direction. The one side was weakening and had lost momentum. "Pull!" shouted the second captain, and it was all up with the first side, for the rope was crossing the line, pulling everyone with it. There would be a great good-natured cheer, but as it was best two-out-of-three, the contest was never over until everyone was exhausted.

The end of the tug-of-war was usually the time for lunch. The table under the tree would be covered with good things—homemade buns, potato salad, fried chicken, ham, hard-boiled eggs, wieners, sandwiches, pickles, cake, jello, to say nothing of the pails of lemonade, and the freezers of strawberry ice-cream under the table.

The picnic ended with a ball game. After a short rest, one of the fathers marked the bases with potato sacks, and captains were chosen. The strongest school children were on the teams, for they could play in the field and take their turn at bat. The bat was thrown in the air to determine the first inning, and someone called out "Play Ball!"

By four o'clock, when the game was over, there would be no more ice-cream or lemonade or coffee. Shadows would begin to lengthen, and at home there were chores waiting to be done. Everything and everybody was loaded again into truck, wagon, or cars, and the school picnic was over. The children, tired and dusty, perhaps sporting some coloured ribbons, or bunches of wilted wild flowers, usually sang all the way home.

May Queen enthroned, Francois Lake, 1951.

In general throughout the era of the one-room school, the traditional pattern of the school picnic remained remarkably the same, yet there were regional variations. The following description, given by Mrs. Pauline Hewat of Enderby, tells how May 24th was celebrated in the Courtenay region of Vancouver Island:

"I am remembering something that brought us much pleasure. It was the 24th of May celebrations. This seemed the most important day of the year. All the schools in the district would go to the same beach, sometimes Kye Bay, sometimes Little River, Little Bay or Hardy Beach or the Comox Spit. We went in hayracks which the farmers used for hauling hay. They were especially constructed with side-boards on them, very strong side-boards, and these were left on so we could sit in the wagon on loose hay.

"Believe it or not, we didn't go to the picnic in slacks in those days. We went in white dresses, with eyelet embroidery, with ribbons in our hair and ribbon sashes, and white shoes

Maypole dancers, Webster's Corner School.

and stockings. In those days there were no automatic washers. Our mothers scrubbed those by hand and boiled them. Everybody went dressed up.

"The farmers who drove us were chosen because of their teams. They would be matched teams—greys and blacks, and matched bays, and whites of Clydesdale and Percheron stock. Get a picture of it! They were enormous! You just don't see those animals now. They would be groomed right up to the ninth degree, their tails braided with ribbons, their manes groomed and ribbons on their heads. The horses loved it! They had bells on them and they jingled and jangled.

"We started out, strung along the road with just a little distance between the hayracks. There would be Courtenay, and Royston, and Comox, and Sandwich, and Solon, and Knob Hill, and Little River, and Cumberland. Everybody had pet insults that they would hurl at the other schools as they came along. We sang songs, and the horses seemed just as happy as we were. It was a happy, happy adventure.

"When we got to the beach, our mothers and fathers would be there. They had gone ahead in the buggies with their well-groomed horses. The buggies of course would be all polished.

"We would be hungry as soon as we got to the picnic ground, and there on the sand would be spread the white linen table cloths, *not* plastic, white linen! These big table cloths would be about six feet wide and over ten feet long. Think of the washing and ironing that took place! On the table cloths would be spread nothing of a store-bought nature. There would be home-made rolls and bread, potato salads and meats of all descriptions, and other salads and layer cakes that were just gorgeous and pies and cookies. Remember those nice big sugar cookies made with farm butter?

"After lunch we were allowed to run around for awhile on the beach, and investigate. Then there would be races, very simple and not highly organized. All pre-schoolers were allowed to race and each one won a nickel regardless. Oh, a nickel was so much money in those days! And then, of course, the bigger ones got fifteen cents, or maybe a shinplaster, ten cents for second prize and five cents for third. After the races were all over, we were allowed to swim. The beaches were very nice and there would be lots of supervision. We played games after supper in the evening and finally went home in the moonlight. It was a very thrilling day, wonderful to remember! I participated in these trips from 1916 to 1923, and I know my older brothers and sister participated in them years before that.

"The 24th of May was then known as the 'Queen's Birthday' and everyone was very much aware of Queen Victoria. To us she was a very dear old lady, someone special."

Trials & Terrors

A sudden plunge into the unknown could be an exhilarating experience for a young teacher from town. Adventures, if embellished a little, made good letters home. Mother and father might worry, but friends would be fascinated by tales of bears on the trail to the school, or a skunk in the outhouse. After a few weeks passed, however, mother and dad seemed far away, and so did the comfort of familiar surroundings. A kind of culture shock would set in, for even simple everyday activities were different in the country.

Often pupils took the education of these touchingly ignorant town teachers in hand. They taught the teachers how to tie up a horse so it wouldn't pull loose or strangle, how to start a fire with shavings, the use of jar rings to keep rubbers on in gumbo mud, the difference between a coyote and a wolf, how to light the gas lamp without burning down the school, the art of trapping a pack rat, and how to identify head lice.

Undoubtedly animals, wild and domestic, were responsible for most of the fearful encounters of rural teachers. Range cattle, lined up along the road to the school, with the bull among them, could make walking to school a daily terror. Cattle seemed to enjoy licking the windows of one school. The teacher would linger by the stove after school, drinking the last drops of tea from her thermos, and praying they would go before it got dark.

A bull moose, bellowing and pawing the ground while a cow moose grazed on the other side of the trail in a willow thicket, caused one unfortunate teacher to crawl hastily under a barbed wire fence. She ran the rest of the way home, her good leather jacket torn beyond repair.

Bears could be counted on to frighten schoolteachers. Miss Horth, a young Englishwoman who taught in the Blue Nose Mountain School near the settlement of Lavington, is said to have left her position quite hastily, the cause being a big, black bear which peered in the school window.

Fred Willway, who taught at Stevenson's Creek nine miles from Princeton, had a similar experience. It was lunchtime when the children were startled by a strange snorting sound, and there, with his head and shoulders in the doorway, was a brown bear. Just out of hibernation, the bear was attracted by the delicious smell of a pot of soup on the school stove.

"Out the window!" said Mr. Willway, who had fortunately trained the children in fire drill procedures, and all eight of them climbed out and ran for home. There was no more school that day.

A teacher who taught in northern British Columbia describes her encounter with a wolf:

"I had to walk about a mile from the school to my cabin, and part of this, after leaving the Alaska Highway, was through bush. It got dark very early in winter, and I remember it was really cold, my parka covered with frost. I felt something behind me, and turned around to see a big timber wolf on the trail. I knew the worst thing would be to run, so I kept on walking faster until finally he just loped up over the snowbank and disappeared. My knees felt weak and I was really glad to shut the door of my cabin and light a cheerful fire."

An adventure with a wolf had a certain aura of romance. A desperate night with bedbugs is less enthralling, but just as frightening. Evelyn Wallace visited at the home of some pupils on a weekend, but she didn't get much sleep:

"It was an old house and not completely finished. There were lathes across tar paper on the attic walls where I slept. In the middle of the night, I began to hear things falling on the bed. I lit a candle, and there were bedbugs falling from the ceiling. I knew what they were, so I put on my old jumbo sweater and huddled beside the candle all night.

"When I came back on Sunday night, my landlady met me at the door and said, 'Just strip right there. Everything off!' She made me take down my hair and she had a carbolic bath waiting for me. This had happened to other teachers and she wasn't going to have anything like that in her house. That's the closest to desperation I came."

The animal many schoolteachers met first was the horse. While still dazed from a long trip, and somewhat shocked by the rough sleeping quarters in the attic of a ranch house, the teacher would be introduced to a huge and powerful animal with a Roman nose, and told, "This here is your horse. He goes by the name of Buck. You'd better get acquainted."

The relationship between the teacher and the horse would be in deadly earnest. Both seemed to realize this as they sized each other up on the first meeting. It was often a case of "learn to ride or else!" for it might be a long walk to the schoolhouse when the snow was deep and the temperature dropped.

There were horses so broad that it was hard to straddle their backs and stay on at a rough trot, horses that would not cross bridges or go over logs, horses that spooked when the halter rope was loose, horses that bolted home, and some that were extremely stubborn if the teacher wanted to go anywhere but to the barn or the school. In general, however, the horse could not be counted among the true terrors, but rather became a good friend and a great pleasure on weekends.

Some frightening incidents were caused by creeks and rivers overflowing in the spring. A young schoolmaster who taught at the mining town of Coalmont went courting one night, and to reach his destination, had to cross the Tulameen River which, in springtime, was in full spate.

"There was a charming young lady whose family lived in the woods about two miles from the village. I had a wonderful walking lamp made from a can and a candle, called a Bug, and I set out to visit this family on my birthday. Normally it was quite easy to cross the Tulameen on an improvised bridge of wire which was suspended with a couple of boards for a duckwalk. I started across, but the river was really roaring and lapping across the middle of the bridge. A big tree had come down and one big root had caught against the side of this fragile structure so that it shuddered and swayed. I was anxious not to miss my birthday supper so I crossed anyway, the water washing right over my feet. At midnight that night, I thought better about coming back the same way, and that was fortunate. Sometime in the night, the bridge went out."

At Kingfisher in the Shuswap country, the river rose for two successive springs and washed the bridge out, flooding quite an area of bush at the same time. The pupils lived quite close to the school, but the young teacher, Isabel Moore, lived on the far side of the creek. Undaunted, she crossed over the roaring water on a log and continued on through the bush balanced on windfalls.

Marjorie Fulton riding to work at Sheridan Lake School, 1936.

Besides having to deal with natural hazards and wild animals, young inexperienced teachers often encountered local characters who seemed strange and even alarming.

Herbert Dodd, who taught at Alice Siding in the thirties, lived in a little frame house on a rock outcropping near his school. It was very lonely, for there were no near neighbours. One day he had a visitor. A stranger stopped by the side of the school and began to draw diagrams on the school fence with a stub of pencil. Hungry for conversation of any kind, Herbert invited him in to the school:

"'Look,' I said, 'I won't let the children write on the fence, and I won't let you write on it, but if you want to use the blackboard, come on in.' So he did, and I sat down on the front desk and listened. He took a piece of chalk and drew it across the board and said, 'Now this is Heaven and this is Hell . . .' and from there on we had a lesson on a strange religion. I was vastly impressed. As I recall, he was going from place to place selling some sort of homemade attachment to a sewing machine that enabled you to darn stockings. I left this diagram on the blackboard, but in the morning I thought, 'Heavens! If the children see that, they'll think I've taken leave of my senses,' so I got up early and erased it. That was about the only visitor I ever had at Alice Siding."

Skookumchuck was a railway station on the Kootenay River, and here Malcolm McPhee began his teaching career. He was lucky to live with the Cameron family who ran the mill, for the three Cameron boys were companions to him and taught him to hunt. But you had to prove yourself in that part of the country to be accepted. This was particularly true for the schoolteacher.

One day in February, word was passed along that an old Irish prospector named McNair wanted to see the "Dominee," or schoolteacher. As McNair lived about eight or nine miles up the Skookumchuck, this meant a long trek on skis, through deep snow, but the young teacher accepted the challenge and finally arrived at the little nine-by-six-foot shack on the river bank. By the open door of the stove sat McNair, feeding the fire with little logs. The room was smoky, but McNair cleared a little space on the window so he could peer out to see if it was daylight or dark, or if someone was approaching his cabin. Malcolm McPhee remembers his visit with the old prospector:

"We talked for quite a while about his education and my education, and his family back in Ireland and my family. Then he wanted to play me a little tune on his violin. Of course it was jig music, but he handled the violin very nicely and I enjoyed it. As the day began to wane, and as nightfall came crashing down pretty quickly, I felt I'd better get on my skis and head for home. He said, 'Oh no, you can't go yet. Look there, the kettle is all steamed up ready to go,' and with that, he made a cup of tea. He had a large loaf of bread which would make about four of our loaves today, and he sort of hugged it bear-fashion and cut a slice off the big loaf. Then he put some cheese and jam on it, and we had tea. Well, I noticed, listening to one of his taller stories, that on the table which was attached to the logs of the wall on one end there was a little flutter of activity. That was where the cheese was. All of a sudden a little mouse had come running along the logs onto the table. He stood up there on his hind legs, with his two front feet on the cheese, gnawed off a piece. Then back he went. I guess McNair noticed that my attention was diverted, for all of a sudden he grabbed a butcher knife, about the same size as a Sicilian knife, and he said something comparable to 'darn mouse,' wielded the blade, and ended the little mouse's career right there. Then he wiped the Sicilian-type knife on his sleeve, grabbed up the loaf, and said, 'Now teacher, have another slice!' I went home very shortly."

The wild and rough appearance of some local characters, harmless as they may have been, could be frightening to a young woman in her first year of teaching. Agnes Sutherland taught at a small place called Tonkawatla, near the town of Revelstoke. She tells the story of her encounter with one of the local bachelors:

"The school was in deep bush, with great tall trees making it very dark inside. A Bolshevik bachelor kindly came to my aid and lopped off enough branches so that the school was brighter. I was grateful, but alas, this led to romantic ideas. If I met him on the road, he would drop to his knees. I found out later that the fellows in the lumber camp encouraged and coached him. Quite naturally, wishing to be on good terms with the settlers, I was polite to him, and he misconstrued this. Somewhere he had heard the word 'woo.' One evening he turned up at my boarding place. Much to the surprise of my landlord, he walked over to where I was sitting, dropped to his knees, and said, 'I'd like to try "woo" on you.' When I recounted this at home on the weekend, my father warned me, 'You're not going back to that place.'

"Then, to make matters worse, when the Bolshevik reported his lack of progress, the

Teacher Don Smith shows off new found riding skills, Peace River area, 1936.

wretched lumberjacks advised him to see my father personally, which he did, calling at my father's office in town. Then I was in for it. My sisters thought the whole thing was hilarious, but my parents didn't.

"Finally convinced that his efforts to woo me were of no avail, my admirer gave up. However, often when I was walking home from school, he would appear suddenly from the bush, always carrying an axe. Sometimes I wondered what might be in his mind."

The fears and imaginary encounters of some teachers, particularly those who lived alone, were often just the product of loneliness. Rosemary King, who taught in a Doukhobor school at Pass Creek, took the place of a teacher who had died of typhoid fever. Later she became very ill herself, and it was determined that the cause was raw milk. After that Rosemary's school was blown up twice and burned down once, destroying all her books and teaching aids. It was little wonder that she was nervous when, returning home one night, she saw a large, round, black object sitting in front of her door. Eyeing the black thing suspiciously, she backed off and stood a long time with growing fear. The thing seemed to be ticking. At last she edged close enough to see that it was a very large red beet. Somebody had come to visit her and left a "calling card."

This same teacher enjoyed the visits of a dear old Russian gentleman who helped her by chopping her wood. She recalls that one day, during class, the door opened and

"grandfather's bearded face appeared around the corner. From this benign visage came the words, 'Mees Keenk, Mees Keenk, geeve me kees.' I backed off rather hurriedly and my face must have shown dismay. 'Give me kees, give me kees,' he pleaded as I retreated. Had this kindly old man suddenly gone mad? 'Give me kees,' he pleaded, 'kees to basement. I bring wood.'"

It took Rosemary a while to regain composure and go on with the lesson.

A teacher in an isolated spot in northern British Columbia had an experience which was so embarrassing that she told no one about it:

"It was well below zero and the fire in the Yukon heater had gone out. I was far from asleep for I could hear someone or something climbing up the rickety stairs to my living quarters above the school—scrunch, scrunch, scrunch—on the icy steps. I leapt out of bed and stood shivering by the door. Finally after an especially loud thump, I decided to open the door and face whatever it was. I flung it open, and there, hanging on the porch clothesline, was the headless culprit. Frozen stiff and banging against the porch railing was my long woolen underwear.

"No, I didn't see the funny side of it, and I didn't tell the children about it the next day. You see, they would tell their parents and everyone would be delighted. They would say, 'The teacher is scared of her own longjohns.'"

But if the fears of some teachers were imaginary, certainly the isolation was real, and there were some who could not stand it. These were the teachers who simply walked off, disappeared without a word to anyone, and never were heard from again.

Such a one was a young girl who taught at Port Essington, near the mouth of the Skeena River, about the time of World War I. Some teachers enjoyed living in this community, but this teacher found it hard to make friends, and also found it hard to control the large number of pupils in her school. One afternoon she did not return to her boarding place. A search party was organized and combed the area until it was too dark to see. Sometime the next morning the young woman walked up the path to her boarding place, and with a set face, packed all her belongings. Not a single word did she speak. There was no explanation; she simply left town. Some people guessed that she had spent the night in an abandoned chickenhouse, but the truth of the matter remained the teacher's secret.

It is a strange coincidence that in this same village another teacher failed to return home. The tragic fate of twenty-one-year-old Loretta Chisholm is, however, a matter of police record.

One Sunday morning in the spring of 1926, the young teacher decided to walk up the old Rancherie Trail. Rough planks marked the way to an abandoned mill. It was a lovely woodsy area, swampy in places, with small bridges where one could see mink, marten, and beaver. Wild flowers were everywhere and, of course, birds were singing on that morning.

Loretta Chisholm never returned. A search party found her the next day, some distance from the trail, assaulted and strangled. Although a young Indian was convicted of the murder on circumstantial evidence, he was later acquitted. People say that a drifter who had killed a farmer near Houston confessed to the crime much later, but the mystery was never really solved.

Shocking incidents like the murder at Port Essington occur very rarely and, of course, chance alone decreed that the victim in this case would be a young schoolteacher. Nevertheless, rural teachers of that era, particularly in the northern part of the province, talked a great deal about the chilling fate of Loretta Chisholm.

The truth is that many of the frightful encounters of greenhorn schoolteachers were of an imaginary nature. The weird cry of a cougar in the bush, or the thumping of a pack rat in the rafters of a cabin, lost their frightening aspect when explained. The actions of animals, the hazards of the weather, and the eccentricities of some local characters, even situations with some danger, could all be handled sensibly. Teachers who had been two or three years in the country had very few encounters with the unknown.

Romance

"Girls were pretty scarce in this country, and schoolma'ams were a speciality. All they had to do was stay put and they'd be snatched up by some jack-pine savage." The author of these words was Earl Baity—trapper, homesteader, and more lately, columnist for the *Cariboo Observer*. His acquaintance with rural schoolma'ams began early, for he helped his father build a one-room school when he was a boy, reluctantly attended several, and passed his boyhood and married life in the pioneer country around Prince George.

Normal School instructors were aware of the emotional hazards of teaching in such out-of-the-way spots as Earl Baity had in mind. They usually warned their female students about the pitfalls of marrying some trapper or stump farmer and being stuck way back in the bush, raising half a dozen children. Parents worried too, for they knew that rough men of all nationalities were out there in the wilds—fishermen, miners, lumberjacks, cowboys, railwaymen, trappers, and farmers. It was often with sinking hearts that they waved good-bye to daughters who were little more than children, realizing that Margaret, Louise, or Jean might never come home again or, at least, the young woman who returned for a visit would not be the same timid, inexperienced girl that waved good-bye.

A classic case of love at first sight was that of Margaret Seely, who had been thoroughly warned not five minutes before. Margaret's parents lived in New Westminster and had imagined a brilliant future for their daughter, for she had her A.T.C.M. from the Toronto Conservatory of Music. They felt a keen disappointment when she accepted a position at Palling, near Vanderhoof. Schools were scarce, and she had to start somewhere. That first year, Margaret Seely was to live and teach at Long's Ranch.

"The inspector met me at Burns Lake. As we were coming up to the gate of the ranch, a young man was coming down the hill in the other direction on horseback. He had a moose on the back of the horse, some grouse in his hand, and a gun over his shoulder. He looked very romantic in a black cowboy hat and a red checkered shirt. It was hilarious because, just a few minutes before, the inspector had been saying, 'Now, I want you to remember that you girls come up here and marry these fellows because you are lonely and a long way from home. Remember these people don't live the life you're used to and you probably wouldn't be happy if you did marry up here. Keep your wits about you now, and don't fall in love.' 'Oh,' I said, 'getting married is the last thing on my mind. I have a lot of things I

Bachelors beware! Dressed up for masquerade dance at Castlegar, 1936.

want to do.' However, when the young man opened the gate for me, he winked, and I fell, just like that."

It was wartime, and Arthur Long was called up for service almost immediately, but five years later he returned and married the same schoolteacher he had met at the ranch gate. Over the years, Margaret Long has happily contributed her musical talents to the community of Vanderhoof.

Chance decisions often change our lives so that, looking back, we say, "If I hadn't missed that train..." or "If I had said 'no' when he asked me to dance..." or "If I had listened to my father's advice...." Deciding which teaching position to accept was often such a chance decision, and the decision often led to romance and marriage.

Lois Morry picked her school rather as one chooses a number on a roulette wheel. She was just nineteen when she asked advice from Mr. Matthews at the Legislature in Victoria as to a suitable school for a young girl:

"He showed me a map and said, 'Well, I have a school here, and here, and here....' Finally I just pointed at the map and said, 'I'd like to go there.' 'There' was Birch Island which I'd never heard of before.

"On the way there, the trainmen discovered I'd never been in the interior. They said 'You know what's going to happen to you? It happens to every schoolteacher who comes up here. You're going to marry a rancher and that's going to be the end of you.' I laughed because I was just coming for one year and then I planned to go to university and take a journalism course.

"The first year I taught at Birch Island, all the men were too young or too old as so many were overseas, but during the second year, they all started coming back. Of course the whole town turned out to welcome them. Everyone would be on the train platform, so when my future husband got off the train, I was there along with everyone in the community. His mother introduced us on the train platform.

"Well, when I told my friends I was going to marry a rancher, they just laughed and laughed, for I grew up in Victoria, and I was scared to death of animals. They couldn't picture me as a rancher's wife. Luckily, I finally acquired a liking for horses and cattle for we have about a hundred and fifty head, not counting calves, on the ranch."

Betty Patterson, also a Victoria girl, was eighteen years old when she secured her first position as a schoolteacher on Hornby Island in 1921. Her parents were relieved that she would be close enough to come home at Christmas, and also that she would *not* be going up-country where there were loggers and miners.

After travelling by the Esquimalt-and-Nanaimo train to Nanaimo, and then by Tally-Ho to the dock, she boarded the CPR boat, the *Charmer*. The captain informed her at lunch that Hornby was so quiet that the Thursday boat was the one excitement of the week. This was true. Everyone was there on the wharf to have a look at the new teacher, especially the young men.

"I felt very school-teacherish. I had long, laced brown boots and a blue ribbon hat with a turned-up brim, and a tweed suit. On the wharf people were dressed in their ordinary farming clothes. Some members of the Harwood family were there. Two of the Harwood family had married schoolteachers and so people teased me and said, 'Fred's waiting for you.' He was the other Harwood brother, a very nice fellow but much older than me."

That Saturday night there was a hard-time dance to welcome the new teacher, and there Betty met Lee Smith, the man she was to marry. It was certainly not love at first sight for he was dressed as a black mammy with a long dress, black stockings on his arms and stove-black on his face. The next day Lee, who was twenty-four and had been to the war, rode over to the school to help clean up after the dance, and that was the beginning of the romance.

Social life on Denman consisted mostly of musical evenings, but sometimes a group of young people would row across the channel from Hornby to Denman Island, walk to the hall, and dance until dawn. Stormy weather would mean waiting a long time before it was safe to row back.

The following year Lee Smith attended Normal School and became a teacher too. Then, while he taught at Hornby, Betty taught on Denman Island. This led to a curious phase of their courtship. There were only a few phones on Hornby, and sometimes the cable went out and they were cut off. Lee rigged up an ingenious system by which they flashed signals across the channel on Wednesday nights. Lee used a big gas lamp and a shingle, and signalled from the top of the Smith barn, while Betty answered from the bedroom of her boarding place on Denman, with an Aladdin lamp. Everyone tried to break the code, and some felt it was just a practical joke. Betty remembers trying to understand one sentence Lee flashed to her, and impatiently signing off, "Good-night." Later she found the message was one long word, "Quitchabellyachin."

The "blinkaphone," as it was called, served a real purpose when a man was stuck at the Spit, with his tug and log boom, because of a big storm. He asked Betty to send a message to his wife on Hornby Island. After that people believed the "blinkaphone" was authentic.

Another sheltered city girl who found romance during her first year of teaching was Margaret Wilson. Picture her, huddled in her muskrat coat by the old stove in the lobby of the Lakeview Hotel in Williams Lake. It was January 1939, and she was waiting for the stage to Likely, a small mining community near the old ghost town of Quesnel Forks. Margaret was definitely nervous. She had been brought up very strictly in Vancouver by parents who were afraid she would perish in the hinterlands of the Cariboo. Primly reading a book of George Bernard Shaw's plays, she tried not to listen to the language and the wild tales circulating in the lobby of the hotel.

The sixty-five mile trip to Likely lived up to her parents' worst fears, for the roads in January were icy and treacherous, and Margaret's two companions on the stage were "inebriated." A day and a half later, the stage finally pulled in to Likely. As the tired schoolteacher surveyed the little village and the cabin that was to be her home, romance was very far from her mind.

There was not much social life in Likely apart from the beer parlour (which, of course, a schoolteacher would never enter), but there were a good many fine older men eking out a living in depression time by trapping and mining the creek. Margaret sympathized with these old-timers, and on mail days some of them used to drop in to her little cabin for tea and cake. This touch of home was appreciated. Certainly Margaret had no thought of romance, that is, until the dance at Quesnel Forks . . .

"They made a new bridge at the old ghost town of Quesnel Forks, seven miles from Likely, so they thought they'd put on a dance. There were only four women at The Forks, one of them an old Chinese lady whose

'Sparking' 1927 style. Teacher Marguerite Harris and date Clarence Smedley off to a mid winter dance.

husband had come in the early days, so they asked Likely to come down to the dance. They cleared out an old building and put planks down for the floor and that was the dance hall

"I remember it was a cold night with a lovely misty moon. The truck that was bringing the refreshments broke down and there was a great shortage of liquor, so the lady that lived in what had been the old jail made gallons of coffee and we went between the dance and her place. It was cold!

"The drummer played on a stovepipe, one of the Hamiltons played the violin, someone had an accordion, and a young prospector named Gordon played a mouth organ. I danced with him several times, and a truck driver said, 'You don't need to dance *every* dance with him!' Agnes Bailey said, 'Mind your own business!'

"When this Gordon was ready to go home, I said, 'Well, you might as well come to my place for tea with the rest of them when you come for the mail.' The very next Saturday he came. I was sitting in my cabin in a kimona with my hair in curlers writing home when I saw this character coming through an avenue of snow. I nearly scalped myself trying to get out of the curlers, but I couldn't get out of the kimona. Well, we had tea and cake, and he continued to come after that. He chopped enough wood for me every week and took me to the dances."

Margaret Wilson married her prospector, Gordon Murray, on February 14, 1942. Although they lived in Vancouver, the place they loved best was a cabin they returned to every summer on the banks of the Quesnel River at Likely. Gordon died in 1978 and his ashes were sprinkled under some birches on the banks of the river they both loved.

Sheila Johnson's meeting with her future husband soon after her arrival in Meldrum Creek is reminiscent of an old-time western novel: a prim and snippy schoolteacher encounters a down-to-earth cowboy and falls in love:

"Yes, I met my Waterloo at Meldrum Creek! One morning I called in at a ranch to pick up the youngsters that were going to school, and there, sitting in a corner behind the stove was a fellow with a cowboy hat pulled down over his eyes. The lady of the house said to him, 'I'd like you to meet the new teacher.' I took one cursory look at the fellow and said, 'How do you do?' Afterwards, he remarked, 'Huh, the new teacher's a stuck-up little witch, isn't she?'

"That same Howie was the cowboy I used to ride to the dances with. I remember once riding forty miles to a dance, from Meldrum Creek across the hills to Milk Ranch, north of Beecher House. We danced from nine until six in the morning, and then stopped at Beecher House for breakfast and let the horses have their way home.

"Howie and I were married in 1936 and, of course, I had to stop teaching. In those days, no married girl was allowed to teach. Oh, that would be scandalous! The only way a married girl could teach was to become a widow."

Many women schoolteachers married into the old ranching families of the British Columbia interior, and made wonderful ranchers' wives.

One of the early teachers along the old Cariboo Road was Mary Melissa Keenan. She came to the Cariboo from the Kootenay area in 1919. Her own schooling had been in the gold mining town of Sandon where her father was a blacksmith. At the early age of fifteen, Mary began teaching in small Kootenay schools until, in February 1919, she secured a position teaching a handful of children in the log school down near the 114 Roadhouse on the Cariboo Road.

Being of pioneer stock herself, she had no difficulty in fitting into the life at Lac La Hache. She boarded in one of the old roadhouses, the 115, which was run by Archie and Mary McKinley.

It was in the dining room of the 115 that Mary Keenan met her future husband. He was the son of John Wright, who had settled in the Lac La Hache area in 1862, built up a ranch, had six sons and six daughters, and ran the 127 Roadhouse. This is how they met:

"I met my husband in a looking glass. There was a long table in the dining room of the 115. I was sitting at one end and he was sitting way down at the other end. Across the corner of the room was a huge mirror. I looked up and he was staring at me in the glass. I lowered my eyes in embarrassment.

"We carried on our courting by going visiting. We'd go to the 127 where Burt's folks lived, and the 126 where one brother lived, and the 122 where the Forbes lived. When the road was good, we'd go by horseback or buggy, and in the winter, by cutter. I stayed on to get married and we built the place at Meadowbank."

Eight children were born to Mary and Burton Wright. Five of these settled in the area and, like their parents, have become part of the life and history of Lac La Hache.

Another of the early Cariboo teachers who married into a ranching family was Lilly Widdowson. She married Glen Walters of Horsefly whose father, Henry Walters, was the first white child born at 83 Mile House. Lilly, who had been teaching at Big Creek, came to teach at Horsefly in 1924. Glen was making his living by guiding, trapping, and ranching. He claims he brought more grizzly bear out of that country than anyone else, but when it came to getting acquainted with the lovely young schoolteacher, he didn't have such an easy time. The first time he saw her, he had come with a friend to Big Creek after a saddle. Lilly wouldn't even talk to him, as they had been "hitting the bottle a little bit."

In 1927, Glen and Lilly were married and went to live in a cabin in the ranch meadows. Their fiftieth wedding anniversary was held in the Horsefly community hall in 1977; many old-timers were there to congratulate one of the area's favourite pioneers and his schoolteacher bride. One of their four children now operates the original Walters Ranch.

Alice Nichols also married a rancher. She taught at Buffalo Creek, east of 100 Mile House, and ended her career by marrying one of the Stafford boys at Springhouse.

Very few male teachers married and settled into rural communities. This was because teaching in a country school gave little chance for advancement but was looked upon as a stepping-stone to something more important. One nineteen-year-old Victoria boy, Dave Hogarth, went to a school at Big Bar Creek on the east side of the Fraser River, not far from Jesmond. For several years, he batched and then moved to the Grinder Ranch. In the four years he stayed there, he developed a great love for horses and the wild country along the Fraser, but the school inspector finally told him it was time to move on and better himself. He did move back to civilization, but his heart was still over by the Fraser River, and four years later he came back to marry Elsie Coldwell of Jesmond. Although the Hogarths live in Victoria, they have a four-wheel drive and like to return to that country as often as possible.

Marrying schoolteachers seemed to run in the Coldwell family. In 1940, a nineteen-year-old schoolteacher who had just graduated from Vancouver Normal School applied for the Jesmond School. Actually, she had no choice as it was the only school advertising

Christmas dance at Spruce Creek.

for a teacher in the whole of British Columbia. Joyce Chapman's parents were reluctant to let her go, but Joyce went down to the post office at Langley, found out where the place was, and then set out by Greyhound bus to Clinton, then by mail stage to Jesmond, thirty-five miles west of Clinton. A well-known rancher named Henry Coldwell was the secretary of the school board, so it was natural for Joyce to board at the Coldwell ranch. For the first year, Joyce was sometimes lonely for her girlfriends, but then she became engaged to Pete Coldwell. Two years after she came to Jesmond, Joyce married Pete Coldwell, although she recalls that several of the schoolchildren did their best to stop the romance:

"One of the little girls, only she is a grandmother now, told me that she and several others would always make some excuse to ride with Pete and I when we went to the store. They were afraid that if Pete proposed and we got married, I wouldn't be teaching them anymore. It worked in reverse because I married Pete and then came back to teach them again."

Jesmond School amalgamated with Big Bar Creek School and was then called Big Bar School, one of the few remaining one-room schools in British Columbia. Joyce Coldwell returned to teach there after her eight children were old enough. She and Pete still live in the lovely old white ranch house, and Joyce is a very involved and dedicated person in that ranching community. Her story illustrates well the important role which many rural schoolteachers played in B.C.

For the most part, these teachers were a high-minded lot, true pioneers who never looked back or regretted falling in love. Many of the more unusual romances of country schoolteachers will never be told, at least not by the participants. Teachers are a pretty close-mouthed lot when it comes to such things. For example, one local gossip still remembers that, in a certain area, the teacher was spanked by the oldest boy in the classroom, and that he used to help her put on her overshoes. Of course it ended up respectably: they were married and the forceful young man is now quite prominent in the Department of Education.

Who's a tenderfoot here? Teacher Dave Hogarth (left) gets acclimatised to Cariboo living, Big Bar School, 1931.

Indian Schools

There was one teacher in the 1930s whose vision and understanding could have been taken as a model for all teachers of Indian one-room schools. Anthony Walsh was a British immigrant, eking out a living as a fox farmer in the Okanagan, when Father Carlyle of Bear Creek recognized his potential and persuaded him to teach in an Indian school at the head of the lake. Two years later he accepted a position as teacher on the Inkaneep Reserve near Oliver, and there he remained for a decade.

For ten years he entered into the life and thought of the people of Inkaneep, patiently gaining the confidence of the children, and then of their parents. He projected himself into their world and the pattern of life on their reserve, with its seasons for fishing, for gathering fruits, for haying and irrigating, and for rounding up the cattle. Slowly he began to ask about the rock paintings he saw in the hills, and about the legends and history of the village, and the Indian songs he heard the cowboys singing.

The children responded very shyly and cautiously at first, but then, with spontaneity and joy, the children of Inkaneep School began to create things that were truly beautiful. The whole village became involved in remembering songs, recounting legends, and making costumes for dances. The result of this activity was that murals and drawings, created by the children on buckskin and building paper, were shown in the capitals of Europe. The stories and legends became dances and plays that were performed before sophisticated audiences and broadcast over the CBC.

Perhaps the most appealing story concerns three shy little girls, one not yet of school age, who approached the schoolhouse one Saturday and asked the teacher to sit on a rock by the small creek near the school. He was told to hide his eyes until he heard the beat of a drum. There beneath the trees, in a natural amphitheatre, two butterflies emerged and danced for him. Deeply moved, he realized that he was watching a purely creative act.

Although Anthony Walsh later accomplished other notable things and was given an honorary doctorate for his work at Benedict Labre House in Montreal, he felt that his years of teaching in the little school at Inkaneep were the most important of his life. In speaking of his work there, Anthony Walsh once remarked that nothing good comes without reflection. Over the years he came to realize that the Indian people have a completely different "world view," and that the white man's system of education is geared to teach them that their view is valueless.

Christmas concert rehearsal, Hubert School. L to R: June George, Andy George, Dorothy Forsyth, Abby Bolitha, Shirley Bourgon, Fred George.

Walsh was, even in the 1930s, a man ahead of his time. It seems extraordinary that the education of Indian children, who are by nature gentle and obliging, has caused the Canadian government such an embarrassing problem for over a hundred years. After the first Indian Act in 1876, the whole matter was conveniently left to the churches. The Anglicans, the Catholic Oblates and Sisters of St. Anne, the United Church, the Methodists, and the Salvation Army were all involved in Christianizing, civilizing, and educating in the wilder parts of British Columbia.

The first church schools were usually residential, for Indians were semi-nomadic. Children could be sent to these schools without the consent of their parents, by order of justices or by the Indian agent for the area.

These early mission schools took little notice of the cultural background of their pupils. They were considered heathen, so it seemed right to teach them to be good, obedient, and religious. The ability to read and write, and some skills in farming, cooking, and sewing were additional bonuses.

Gradually the churches opened day schools on reserves, usually on a seasonal basis, until finally the federal government accepted financial responsibility for these, and hired teachers to run them. These teachers were picked for their religious leanings, and were paid considerably less than teachers who taught for the provincial government. This sometimes attracted poor teachers who could not get positions elsewhere. However, many of the teachers were devout and dedicated people who had grown to love the quiet serenity of reserve life and the trusting, obedient children. The real drawback was the lack of training. Many teachers were not on the same wavelength as their students, mistaking shyness and silence for lack of intelligence, and ignoring the rich Indian history and folklore to regale the mystified children with European nursery rhymes and fairy stories. Ironically, "Red Riding Hood and the Wolf" might be told in the story hour, while the local story of a man who took a wolf's form and could communicate if met on the trail, would be considered strange and rather spooky.

Many years after Anthony Walsh taught at Inkaneep, a teacher arrived at the small Indian village of Moricetown on the Bulkley River.

Teacher Ann Evans and Indian students, Skeena Valley, 1940's.

In the 1950s this village, although not geographically remote, seemed cut off from reality, and the teacher felt isolated and sad despite the beauty of the surroundings. In the winter it was very cold. Smoke rose straight up from the log houses, and stars seemed very close and brilliant. In those days there was one street down which the log buildings straggled; this was called Jackpine Street. There were several totem poles, but the only public buildings were the tumbledown log school, the hall, and the Catholic church. Two miles away, by the railway, was a store owned by a white man.

Over 150 years ago, Moricetown was the one important village on the river. Below the village were the falls, ancient fishing grounds of the Carrier Indians. Salmon ascended in huge shoals then, and there were houses on both sides of the river, and a dam. The Indians were well off; each clan chief had his own fishing stand on the river and his own hunting grounds. People traded their furs and hides with coast Indians for shells and copper and oolichan grease. Wonderful stories of historic battles, dreams, and visions were handed down; stories of which white people knew very little.

About 1820, a landslide partially blocked the Bulkley, and many people moved further downstream and settled in a village called Hagwilget. Now there were two Carrier villages, and the one which later took its name from the famous Oblate missionary, Father Morice, began to decline. Fishing was not so good, there was a smallpox epidemic, and white settlers levelled big areas of forest for farms and settlements. Finally the logging industry finished the hunting, and the railway came in.

The schoolteacher who taught in Moricetown in the early fifties tells of her shocked and inadequate response to life in this once prosperous village:

"It had been the custom for the Indian Department to hire Catholic teachers for that reserve, but the former teacher (who it was said had been bootlegging) left at Christmas. I was casting around for a vacancy anywhere and was hired. Nobody enlightened me that the people of Moricetown did not really like white people, and I was completely ignorant of their history and culture.

"The Moricetown school of that time was a dilapidated log building whose ceiling and walls did not keep out the weather. Rain and

Students and teachers, Sechelt Indian Residential School.

thawing snow dripped steadily onto the floor in spring, and in cold weather, snow drifted through the cracks between the logs. The log house which stood at the edge of the clearing at the end of Jackpine Street, and which served as a teacherage, was in a like state. Part of the roof fell in one cold winter night and dumped snow on the bed.

"The day after I arrived in Moricetown, an unfeeling and bitter doctor visited the school. He was a displaced European who had been assigned to the Hazelton area to serve the Indian population. The doctor looked down the children's throats, and then showed me a dirty and littered shelf in the teacherage. He informed me that this was medicine and that I was in charge of first aid. As I knew nothing of first aid, this was a frightening assignment. Serious flu cases, chopped-off fingers, and baby convulsions were not discussed at great length in the little first-aid manual.

"Later, a German dentist arrived. She stayed in the teacherage and, while there, pulled tooth after tooth using a mechanical foot drill. One of the older girls worked the drill with her foot while the doctor cried out in exasperation, 'Gott in Himmel, pump!' and blood splattered on the floor. I thought the children very brave, and wondered why they could not have gone to a dentist's office in Hazelton, but I never thought to complain on their behalf.

Ann Evans' students in Skeena country. Evans and her husband Hubert spent six years among Indian villages of the Skeena in late forties and early fifties. Their experiences are described in Mr. Evans novels Mist on the River *and* Son of the Salmon People.

"Eighteen or twenty children came to school faithfully when circumstances allowed. That was a bad winter for flu and children coughed steadily, huddled closely around the stove in the mornings, sitting on sticks of wood with their coats and mitts still on. The wood was green and the fire burned reluctantly.

"Speaking English was a problem for the smaller children and progress was therefore slow; however, everyone really wanted to learn to read and everyone tried. We had Catholic readers, but the pictures must have seemed strange to the children—scenes of fair-haired families with front lawns, and sidewalks, and cars, and Daddy coming home from work. On Friday afternoons, the priest came to give Catechism. The children called out the answers together while I sat outside on the steps.

"We had little parties, with gramophone music and games, and in the spring, a picnic with the Hagwilget School children. However, these little pleasures hardly seemed to be an antidote for such essential sadness. The cause of the sadness, I thought in my ignorance, was drinking, for heavy drinking was a fact of life in Moricetown.

"Shortly after I arrived, there was a dance in the hall, and I went, hoping to meet some of the parents and to feel less lonely and cut off. When I pushed the door open, I did not see a scene of friendly gaiety. The hall was lit by gas lamps, and on the stage two saxophone players played a never-ending tune. No one was dancing, but several of the schoolgirls were reeling around the door, balanced on highheeled shoes. On a bench against the wall, an old lady held her son's head, and rocked back and forth wailing. There was a considerable amount of blood, and the stove was knocked over. As I, the teacher and first-aid person, ignominiously retreated, there on the road, beneath a beautiful cold and starry sky, one man was hitting another with a two-by-four.

"Aside from first-aid calls, my contacts with adults were few. One cold winter night I answered a knock at the door, thinking it was probably a call for first aid. An old man, wrapped in a tattered blanket, came in. Perhaps his mind was wandering for we both stood and looked at one another until finally an owl hooted behind the house. 'You've got a bad friend,' he said. 'Some people here's going to die.' He spoke for himself for, within a week, he was dead.

"I remember, too, an old lady who stepped out of her house and invited me in for a cup of tea. We could not speak the same language, but I still remember how kind she was . . . the sort of person one thinks of as a comforter.

"A young couple visited me several times. By the light of the coal-oil lamp they told me stories that seemed more real than all the stories in the children's readers. I learned by these stories how closely human and animal life is bound together in the world of the Indian, and how all the natural landmarks—mountains, streams, and rocks—are like animate beings. I still have the notebook in which I wrote down these legends of the Carrier people.

"The year I taught at Moricetown, the government Fisheries Department was putting in a fishladder at the Falls, ancient fishing grounds of the Moricetown Indians. It is not surprising that the Indians felt this as a violation. The tin roof of the temporary government camp presented a visible target, and someone took several shots at the roof from the forested hillside above. But several potshots are not an adequate response to a hundred years of destruction of a culture.

"The Fisheries Department, in good faith, invited everyone in the village to a feast at the camp. There were plenty of refreshments, and some people got very drunk. There was some trouble. The friendly gesture on the part of the Fisheries Department was also inadequate. Too much water had gone over the Falls.

"After I left Moricetown, I felt sorry that I had not stayed and been of some help to the children. Perhaps if I had known more about their way of thinking, I could have talked to the children and their parents about things that really mattered to them. At any rate, I was not up to it and I left in June with a feeling of sadness."

The same teacher drove through the village of Moricetown some thirty years later. It was September and people were fishing from the rocks below the falls, but there were some visible changes in the village. The old log school, the hall, and the teacherage had fallen down or burned down. There was a large community hall, a firehall, a store, and many more people and cars—but no school. The children, she was told, were all bussed in to school in Smithers, hustled into a larger world, like so many country children, ready or not.

Most provincial one-room schools used to have a scattering of Indian children attending, and often they fitted in quite happily with white children. However, the popular myth that children just naturally get along together is not always true. A lone Indian child in a room full of self-assured rancher's children might feel as out of place as his teacher would at a loggers' convention. There are teachers who tell of children who utter not a single word all year except "yes" and "no." This awesome silence is not sullenness or stupidity, but self-protection.

A small girl who longs to draw on the blackboard with coloured chalk at recess, might send her sister to ask for the chalk while she stands with her back turned. "What's the matter with your tongue, Lucy? Can't you speak for yourself?" the teacher asks sharply. The child hangs her head. How is the teacher to know that, in the child's culture, it is bad manners to ask directly?

Cathy Mulvahill, a Chilcotin rancher's wife, was teaching in the one-room school at Chezacut in 1980. Attendance varied, but her

Sister Pat Bennett with students at Kamloops Indian Residential School, 1968. School closed next year.

register listed eighteen pupils. In this case, the white children were in the minority as there were sixteen Indian children, two whites, and two mixed. Mrs. Mulvahill understood and identified with the children she was teaching. Commenting on the absence of some of the children from the classroom she said, "These people are still semi-nomadic. The diet is mostly deer, moose, and fish. When the fish are running they will go and dip salmon and dry them. Right now there is a family away hunting. They have taken all the children. That's quite understandable. That's their way of life, and you work around it."

Because of Mrs. Mulvahill's belief in the value of accomplishment, she and the children were busy with some interesting projects. The children had made a beautiful quilt after collecting, washing, carding, and spinning wool. Their next project involved digging spruce roots and weaving baskets in the old way so that the baskets would hold water.

But the most unusual project undertaken at the Chezacut School had a very practical result. It had to do with the use of logs:

"Around the school are basically four types of sample fences that are common in the Chilcotin. One is a snake fence, one is a log fence with a spacer, the third is a Russell fence, and fourth is a stake-and-rider or buck fence. That is used mostly around Anaheim Lake. It looks as though it is on a slant and it confuses the moose. Moose have very long legs and can go over most fences. These sample fences were built by an Indian. The children and he went out and cut the logs, peeled them, and then he showed them how to build them."

They also constructed a log cabin:

"This cabin in the school yard was to show the children how to build a log house. I wanted to encourage their parents who still live in tents to build their own houses. It has had a great effect."

Although Cathy Mulvahill believes that each child is a precious individual, she also believes that the rich cultural background of Indian children, as well as the realities of their present way of life, should be understood by teachers.

There could be no sharper contrast to these views on Indian education than those expressed by the federal government in 1969 in the controversial "White Paper." This document stated bluntly that Indians were no different than other Canadians and should not be treated differently. The Indian people, far from being flattered, called the "White Paper" genocidal.

In line with their new policy, the Indian Department contracted with the provincial government so that Indian children could be bussed into towns to attend public chools. The last Indian residential school was closed in 1974, and today there are very few schools, one-room or otherwise, left on Indian reservations.

But there is light at the end of the tunnel. After all the blundering, educators are recognizing that the thinking and background of Indian children from reserves is different enough to make many of the tests and much of the curriculum of the public schools seem alien to them, especially when they are encountered in the stressful environment of a town classroom. In 1977 the Department of Education at U.B.C. added courses to its curriculum that were especially designed for those who plan to teach Indian children, in particular, for the growing number of native teachers.

At the same time, the Native Indian Brotherhood published a brief called "Native Control of Indian Education." The ideas in this brief were demonstrated on several B.C. reserves, the first two of which were Mount Currie and Bella Bella, where the band councils contracted to run their own schools. Similar experiments were then planned, one being on the Nishga Reserve, within the provincial school system. The exciting thing is that Indian people are now making decisions about the education of their children, whether this be in grade schools with Indian teachers in charge, or in town schools where special courses can be offered to Indian children.

As for the little schools on reservations: for better or worse, like all country one-room schools, their number has dwindled and they have all but disappeared.

Doukhobor Schools

Teaching in the one-room schools in the Doukhobor villages of the Kootenay and Slocan Valley areas presented a special challenge, and an experience akin to no other in the province. Although most teachers who lived among the Doukhobor people in the early days speak with admiration of their integrity and high ideals, it must have been difficult to be plunged suddenly into a culture so foreign to the Canadian way of life. In addition, the Doukhobors were deeply suspicious of Canadian officialdom, and they were filled with resentment at the ruling that their children must be educated in the Canadian school system.

To understand their obstinacy and their mistrust of anyone in authority, it is necessary to know the background of the events that drove them to this stand. The Canadian Doukhobors, or "Spirit Wrestlers," came from a group of people in Russia, formed to follow the teachings of three brothers, "Cossacks of the Don," who led them away from the Orthodox Russian Church to worship "God in Spirit and Truth." By 1806, this "Christian Community of Universal Brotherhood" was constantly subject to persecution, its members confined to cruel prisons and life imprisonment in the mines of Siberia. In 1821 a Caucasian chief attempted to separate 2,500 children of the sect from their parents, so that they might be induced to give up their religion and return to orthodox society (a surprising parallel to events which took place in B.C. in 1953).

In spite of continual persecution and suffering, these people clung together with an unswerving belief in the communal principle as a way of life. They were firm pacifists—against militarism, patriotism, and the killing of any animal life. They could not fit in to any of the organized societies in which they attempted to settle, and they were harried from place to place, finally coming out to Saskatchewan in 1898. Their troubles were by no means over.

When Peter "The Lordly" Veregin (not to be confused with his successor, Peter Veregin the Second) came out to Canada in 1902, he discovered a split in the sect's ranks. Between 1909 and 1912 he brought most of the true believers to B.C., to establish communal farms

Warehouse school at Doukhobor town of Brilliant, 1932. Teacher Pauline Romaine, who also lived in building, wryly notes, "The ventilation was excellent." Below: *Romaine with class of Brilliant boys.*

in the Kootenays. By 1909 there were many prosperous settlements: Brilliant, on the Columbia River three miles from Castlegar; Glade, east of Brilliant; Grand Forks; Pass Creek, fifteen miles north of Brilliant; North Fork of the Kettle; Champion, south of Brilliant; Crescent Valley; Slocan River; and west of Nelson on the Kootenay.

For a while, all went well with them. They were hard workers and good farmers, and soon the Kootenay farms prospered with well-irrigated orchards and the community had some $4.5 million in assets, and few debts. Still, they could feel no allegiance to the country which sheltered them. Peter the Lordly maintained that the Doukhobors had been led to believe that, by acquiring title to B.C. lands from private individuals, they had no obligation to obey the laws of individual registration of land titles, and of registration of births and marriages. They also claimed exemption from the Public Schools Act.

For some time, no attempt was made to send the children from the Kootenay settlements to school, but finally, under pressure from the school authorities, the Doukhobors agreed that the children of Grand Forks settlement should attend the public school. They also agreed to build a schoolhouse in Brilliant settlement. After one term they closed this school, and in less than a year they withdrew their children from Grand Forks School.

This action precipitated the forming of a Royal Commission on Doukhobors in 1912 to study the situation. They found that there were, in one area, over 700 school-aged children not attending schools. The reasons given by the parents were many and varied, and in some cases, startlingly logical. When the commission was in Brilliant, one old woman, through an interpreter, said that one of the reasons the parents objected to sending their children to school was that the teacher, a lady, curled her hair and wore ribbons. The parents noticed that, after the girls had been attending school for a few weeks, they began to curl their hair. They thought this was such a terrible evidence of vanity that they refused to subject children to the teacher's degrading influence.

The Doukhobors were, in the main, an agricultural people, and their work on the land was all important. The commission found that in the whole community of 7700 people, there were only about twenty who could converse in English, read a paragraph in a newspaper, or write a letter. They objected to educating their children because they claimed that it would cause them to leave the soil and engage in commercial pursuits. One small boy, John Masloff, asked permission to say a few words to the commission for himself and his fellow children. He stated that they had been attending public school for ten months, but did not wish to go to school again because the teacher who had taught them—although she had been very kind to them and they loved her—belonged to the people who had put their friends in jail.

In a well-prepared brief, the Doukhobors asked: Was it not a fact that Canadian children, when educated, would not work on the land? Did not schools educate children to accept military service and believe in the sinful business of war? Did not teaching lead to expediency of easy profit, thieves, cheaters, and exploiters of the working class on earth? Did it not mean that as soon as a person reads and writes, they then leave parents and relations for unreturnable journeys on all kinds of speculative depravity? Did not crack-brained officials attain to highest universities where Glory to God is not admitted? Did not well-educated people swallow down all the common people? So powerfully did they put their case that one wonders why non-Doukhobors did not remove their children from the schools en masse!

At about the time of this commission, extremists, later known as "Sons of Freedom," began to separate from the Orthodox Doukhobors. While the majority of the sect were probably willing to accept the gradual infiltration of schools into their neighbourhoods, the Sons of Freedom were passionately and violently against it.

By the 1920s there were eleven small schools in the area, but only about half the children attended them. The government attempted to force attendance, holding the local school boards responsible for enforcing the attendance law. The costs, over and above the government grants for schools, were charged against the Doukhobor properties. The extremist faction became more active, and by 1923 there began a long series of protests including arson, bombings, and nude parades. The first destruction of a school occurred in the razing by arson of the little school at Outlook.

After Peter the Lordly was killed, blown up by a bomb on a train in 1924, the violence increased. In 1925 there were nine schools burned to the ground, and though the majority of orthodox Doukhobors were now complying with the school laws, the Sons of Freedom continued to burn and bomb schools.

In 1929 four more schools were burned. The next year Krestova School was burned, with the teacher barely escaping in time. In 1931 the Champion Creek School was bombed; if the teacher had not happened to be at the opposite end when the blast went off, she could easily have been killed. Three previous schools on this site had gone up in smoke.

By May 1932, recurring truancy, vandalism, arson, and bombings forced the government to take another firm stand. Defiance, in the form of nude parades, landed 600 in jail, and the Children's Aid Society cared for the children in Vancouver. When the Freedomites were released in 1935, however, little effort was made to enforce the attendance laws.

Progress of children in the schools dominated by Freedomites was negligible. As soon as a child showed progress, he was removed from school until his newly-learned skills were forgotten. A few very bright youngsters were allowed to attend school regularly, and the teachers were delighted until they learned that they were being trained to be future leaders of the community.

In 1947 a Royal Commission under Harry J. Sullivan stated that:

"Taking school to the Doukhobors made arson too easy. It is hard to obtain the services of good teachers for these isolated schools since the problem of finding suitable boarding places, and the actual fear of fanaticism are very real concerns. These small one-room schools make it difficult for a child to advance further than Grade Eight, with the result that very few have the opportunity to mingle with English speaking children of their own age."

In 1948 and 1949 the situation was so bad that armed guards watched over the tiny schools in the Kootenays twenty-four hours a day, at the cost of $77,446 a year.

A 1952 research committee under D. Hawthorne found that 300 Doukhobors were not attending school. It was decided that higher salaries should be paid teachers in "areas

Photos taken by teacher Pauline Romaine after the school she was teaching in at Glade was bombed, June 1936.

Mountain of mourners turn out for burial of Peter the Lordly Veregin, 1924.

resistant to education," and that flexible programs of studies be devised for use in such areas.

In 1953 violence continued and there were 400 burnings. A number of Doukhobors moved to Perry Siding in the Slocan Valley and set up a tent town near the school. To embarrass the authorities, they marched up to the tiny one-room school, capable of housing fifteen pupils, and presented 100 school-age children to be enrolled. Then they staged a dramatic nude parade near the schoolhouse.

It was in 1953 that eighty-five Sons of Freedom children were rounded up and committed to a vacant sanatorium in New Denver, as welfare problems. The first three months were a nightmare for the children and for their teacher, John Clarkson. The children were hostile and rebellious, resisting any form of participation, vandalizing the premises, smashing the windows and flooding dormitories. Then, at last, there was a breakthrough. After days of forced attendance in the classroom, they suddenly evinced a craving for education, and devoured every bit of knowledge presented to them. They showed an astonishing ability to work, and many proved to have extraordinarily high I.Q.s. The children became happy and co-operative, and the parents realized that their children were being well cared for. After seven years, the parents promised that if they were sent home, the children would all attend schools near their villages. It was a promise kept, and Freedomite children attending Kootenay schools had a higher attendance than non-Doukhobors.

Through all these years of turmoil the Sons of Freedom children had been used for publicity stunts; they had been dragged on protest marches and demonstrations. Through it all, they were torn between their parents' hatred of the government, their own desire for learning, and their often genuine love of their teacher. The teachers, during these troubled times, found the children to be "beautiful, well-behaved youngsters with a sweetness and gentleness in their faces. They seemed intelligent and eager to learn, healthy, spotlessly clean, and very well-mannered. Then, by the time they were ten or twelve, their faces would begin to reflect the suspicion and resentment of authority learned at their own homes."

And what of the teachers who ventured into these alien areas to attempt to teach these children to read and write English, and perhaps to love their new Canadian heritage? On the whole, they found the Doukhobor people to be kindly and hard working, and deeply devoted to their children. The challenge they had to meet was the firm resistance to education as we know it, the loneliness of living among a people with totally different values, and the immense task of being the only Canadianizing influence in the community, of attempting to alleviate the suspicion and dislike of outside authority so deeply implanted in these people's hearts.

The teachers seldom knew security. While the radical Doukhobors never deliberately harmed a teacher, some had very narrow escapes. While bombings and arson usually took place when it was assured that the teacher was away for the weekend, she never knew when she might return to find her school burned to the ground and her investment of books and personal belongings in ashes.

In some cases, the teacher had a room in one of the large community houses. These were square red brick buildings, built in pairs per hundred acres, with thirty to fifty people living in buildings behind the houses. Downstairs there was a large sitting room with tables and benches around the room. This sometimes served as the schoolroom. There were from eight to ten bedrooms in each house, and one of these was converted to living quarters for the teacher. Each house contained a large kitchen-dining room with a long dining table and benches where the community members gathered and ate their meals together. At the back, about thirty or forty feet from the houses, were the living quarters of the other members of the group, bath-houses, store houses, and a soup kitchen where some of the cooking was done.

The teacher was occasionally invited to share the communal meal, but usually she cooked her own meals in her small room. In most cases, she had no social life of her own, nor was she welcomed into the community life. It was a lonely and isolated position, and the nearest town or village was usually inaccessible during the week. Alone in her bare little bedroom she would prepare the next day's lessons, or stand at her small window, looking out over the miles of neatly cultivated fields, to the brown rolling hills, or down to the river, winding along in the distance through its deeply cut chasm.

Freedomite students in converted barn, Krestova, 1959. Teacher Volodya Stepano (bending over) taught only 3 R's—and in Russian. Parents' efforts to retain old ways are apparently lost on boys at back, who are breaking out in Elvis Presley hair do's.

Floating Schools

British Columbia's west coast is fringed with steep mountains and rocky shores. An unending forest stretches from waterline to mountain top. The travelling, or "gyppo," logging outfits which set up their camps in the bays and inlets indenting this rugged coast sometimes found the terrain so steep that there was no room for buildings on the shore. Camps were often constructed on log floats or rafts that could be towed from one area to another. These camps had one foot on land and the other in the sea.

Loggers who worked these isolated camps were a hardy bred. There were Norwegians, Finns, Swedes, Danes, Poles, and many other nationalities working together. Teachers who taught in float schools met all types.

It was on a float school at O'Brian Bay that Edna Davis began her teaching career. Although she had written many job applications that year, by January she was still without a school and was feeling discouraged. Then one day she received a phone call which changed her life:

"Early in 1931 my friend Jessie, who had already accepted a school in Fort St John, phoned me and said, 'Would you like a school, a small school?' Well I thought she said the school was on a slope, and I said, 'Yes, I'll take anything!'

"It all sounded fine to me. Then I found out the school was at O'Brian Bay—not on a slope, but on a float! My mother laughed because I had said, 'Gee, I hope I don't get a school away off in the interior somewhere.' It

Up the coast everything came by water, especially school children. These Pender Harbour students pose in their dugouts and kicker boats in front of the Donley Landing School, 1925. Later the local school board established a gasboat service which lasted into the 1960's.

was intriguing to me because I love the water and so I ended up with a school and all the buildings on floats.

"I went over on the CPR ferry to Vancouver and then down to the good old Union Steamship docks. I took one look at the old *Venture*, a real old freight boat with rust on her sides, and wasn't too sure whether it was going to make it. The *Venture* was later sunk on her way to China.

"We got aboard, and of course there were many loggers going back up to the camps after their little sprees in town. I had never seen a person that I knew was drunk, and that was quite an experience in itself. I really felt that I was living, you know.

"We left Vancouver on a Monday and we didn't arrive at O'Brian until Wednesday. It seemed as though we travelled miles and miles, and we did—up and down the long inlets. We went all the way up to the head of Knight Inlet and down again, and we were in the same place as we were the day before.

The boat was delivering freight and mail to all the logging camps and everyone came down to meet the boat, as it came in just once a week. There was no refrigeration so people had to order things that travelled well. Sometimes things arrived in such a state they could almost walk off the boat.

"It seemed a long way into the unknown . . . miles and miles from civilization, past mountains and fjords with seagulls crying.

"So we sailed through Kenneth Pass and up to McKenzie Sound and O'Brian Bay. The mail and freight were off-loaded and we were met by the husband of the lady I travelled with, and another jolly fellow. I wrote to my mother later that he was something like off a sardine can. Remember the picture of the bearded man with a sou'wester hat? This man had a steam boat, one of the few steam boats on the coast. It was his children that I was going to teach. The lady of the house was British, a short, stout, little woman with red cheeks. She had three children with her. The fourth was so shy that I didn't meet him until the next day.

"The house on the float wasn't very fancy, but it had several bedrooms and a kitchen. There was decking around it, there was a float for storing wood, and then my schoolhouse on another float which I reached by walking along planks. It was a two-room building. A blacksmith shop was on another float. There were gill-pokes to the shore to keep the floats from going aground when the tide went out.

"There were two other families on separate floats, both former teachers who had come up there. One had married Mr. R's brother, and one had married his nephew. There weren't any relatives left for me to marry, so I had to marry outside the family!

"The children were not quite like city children for they had lived all their lives up there on the floats. Some of the children didn't learn to swim until they were grown up, yet they didn't wear life-jackets and were in and out of the boats all the time. Mrs. R felt that if the children learned to swim they'd get careless. The boy that was so shy, years later joined the army and became a top swimmer.

"The schoolhouse was nice and clean. It was really the kitchen part of my house, with a sink and kitchen table and chairs. There was a small blackboard on the wall and a big heater. The other room was my bedroom. I was really lucky to have such a nice place to go to.

"Bachelors from the different camps would come over to see what the new teacher looked like." O'Brian Bay in the 1930's.

"These people had been trying to get a public school going, but they needed enough students, and it was hard to find some place for the children to board. The family had decided to hire a teacher and pay her themselves. Well I think that I got twenty dollars a month and board. I remember looking at another school up there and realizing if I paid my fare up and my board, I wouldn't have anything left over. At least, this way I got something.

"There were four children in my school, and four grades. I religiously followed the course of study that we were given at Normal School. When I ran into snags, I improvised. The children had had different experiences than city children. They were more knowledgeable about some things, such as fishing and tides and logging, but not about some things in the course of studies. They had been out to the city once and didn't like it. Even to this day, the older girl goes to Vancouver and wants to get back as soon as possible. The other people in the area like to go to town but are glad to get home.

"I really fitted in. I tried to adjust my way of life to theirs. The thing that I found the hardest, outside of not having anyone to talk to about the school, was the fact that you never escaped the children. I was boarding with the family, eating with the family, and there was nowhere to walk except on the float. I like the water so I learned to row. But then when I borrowed the boat the kids would all say, 'We'll come with you Miss Davis.' It was a little hard on discipline, because mother was a little severe. If the teacher had been after one of the children they were liable to get a licking at home. This was the most difficult thing; to discipline the children, not to get too friendly, and yet to fit in with the family life too.

"The boat came in once a week, and boat-day was a big day. It was like going to town. O'Brian Bay wasn't a town, but it had a store, a post-office, a big warehouse, some gas tanks, and a bootlegger around the corner in one of the big bays. We were quite a distance away, but going for the mail on a Wednesday was the big treat of the week.

"You had to make your own amusements. We did a lot of reading. Mr. R read a great deal and had a lot of interesting books. He was a great conversationalist too, so we spent a lot of time chatting.

"On the week-end, bachelors from the different camps came over to see what the school teacher looked like. There was another family that lived across McKenzie Sound and I rowed over and visited them.

"Well, I finally had a boy friend of course. He used to take me for rides in a speed boat. This was something new, as there were only gas boats then. We'd go down to O'Brian Bay or Claydon Bay.

"There were big dances periodically, but it took a long time to get to the dances. The only one I went to was at Stako's Island at the mouth of Kingcome Inlet, and it took quite a running time to get there. You'd start on a

Saturday morning, and then sometimes you wouldn't get back till late Sunday. You'd dance all night, have breakfast in the cookhouse, and get back in time to go to bed. People from all the camps would come, and teachers who had gone up the coast and married loggers, and fishermen. There was quite a bit of drinking went on.

"I remember one well-educated man, a black sheep of his family who lived in the bush . . . he came to the dance. I wore a white dress and he left black finger marks on the back of it.

"It was a treat when the Columbia Mission boat came in. They had a padre on board, and we'd go aboard for the service. I even played the organ once. They had a so-called lending library. I tell you the books were of ancient vintage, sent out by dear old ladies in England for the impoverished natives. They had a doctor on board and he would check all the ailments. Our closest hospital was at Alert Bay, across the Queen Charlotte Sound, three or four hours steady running in good weather. If the Westerlies came up you just didn't go. We had no radio telephones then.

"My husband, my boy friend then, lived inside the 'Roaring Hole,' and could only come out on certain tides, so sometimes our courtship was cut a bit short when he had to catch the tide. The Roaring Hole was further up McKenzie Sound, a very narrow passage, and you could just go in at slack tide. There was only one boat that tried to run the tides and the fellows drowned. Sometimes Tobe would miss the tide, and I'd jump off his boat onto the boat of people working there, and he'd tear along and try to catch the tide. Sometimes he'd have to stay outside the Roaring Hole and wait for the next tide.

"I lived for almost twenty years up the coast. I was married at Trimble Cove, which is just off McKenzie, so I went right back to

Perhaps the most elaborate of all the floating communities in the twenties and thirties was Simoom Sound, near Kingcome Inlet. The floathouse shown here was originally the Simoom Sound school.

One of the proudest boasts of Simoom Sound was the massive floating ballfield citizens built for the local schoolchildren.

Inside the Simoom Sound School. Teachers could almost dream they were safely ashore, except for an occasional rocking motion.

the scene of the crime. I lived on a float all my married life and raised three children. I taught my own children.

"We had a school there for two years in the community dance hall that we built. It was on a float, and we even had a badminton court on a float, and that was the play ground for the children. Later I'd row my daughter across the bay to school every morning and pick her up at night.

"It was a good life. People were very friendly, the forest wardens and fish wardens and our friends. Even if we didn't see them for three months they were still our friends. No one came to visit for just an hour. They came for the weekend because it was such a long run.

"Yes, there was a great deal of closeness! When you were married you had nowhere to go to get away from your husband. You couldn't go for a walk, but I'd say, 'I'm going for a row!' and he'd push the boat away very gladly. I'd row like fury across the bay, and then I'd just drift back home to the float."

Dora White had a very different experience teaching on a float school, for hers was anchored off a small Indian settlement on Village Island, at the mouth of Knight Inlet. The people were called Mamalilacullas, and were of the Kwakiutl tribe.

"I went over to Village Island from Alert Bay on the Indian agent's boat. In the tiny village, I found I was to stay with two Anglican missionaries who lived on a float. One of them, Miss O'Brien, had personally financed the building of the little school and she owned the float-house where we lived. Miss O'Brien was not there when I arrived for she had gone to England as her sister was ill, but I stayed with the other missionary, Miss Dibben.

"School didn't start until October, for the Indian women worked in the canneries up Knight Inlet, and the people who owned the fish canneries wanted them to work as late as possible in the season. When I first arrived, there were only about six children, but then more and more came to school as the families returned, but not always the same children. Organizing the school work was difficult. One Monday, several didn't come, and when I went to find out why they were absent, they said they thought it was Sunday. The following Monday, I had completely different kids. The others had all gone off with their families to gather sea gull eggs. Then the herring were running and some went off to get herring. All the children were in different grades as well, so it took a lot of planning.

"Before I went to Village Island, the inspector, Captain Barry, helped me make out a list of everything I might need. He had every Indian school in B.C. to inspect. I remember when he first came to Village Island. It was a rainy day. He was a heavy-set man and didn't like walking on those slippery floats. He no sooner got on our float when Miss Dibben gave him a blast because I hadn't been paid. The Department of Indian Affairs paid ninety dollars on a quarterly basis, but they didn't see fit to send my cheque until the middle of March. Of course there was no place to spend money anyway, and Miss Dibben boarded me until I got paid, but that first Christmas I had no money for Christmas presents.

"The float-house had been a bunkhouse, and then a little room had been added here and a little room there, and it was tied up to the beach. When the tide came in and out, one end of it went up in the air and down. Once it caught fire. Some of the men who had been logging were just coming past our place to go to the village, and without explaining, one of them came running into the house. He said, 'Miss Dibben, where's your water bucket?' To our astonishment, he filled the bucket and poured water down the chimney.

"The little frame houses of the village were built along the waterfront. On the side of the path near the beach, they were up on piles. Behind the houses was heavy bush of cedar and salal. We could hear wolves for they came across the island chasing the deer. When I rang the little bell at the school for church service, all the dogs in the village would howl and the wolves would howl back.

"The Mission boat came over once a week. When people were ill, we used to wait and wait for the boat to come in. There was a really nice doctor who went from house to house with Miss Dibben.

"The first year I taught there, Miss Dibben broke her ankle at the end of November. One of the families had a gas boat so we took her the sixteen miles to Alert Bay. You learn about first aid at Normal School, so I put a splint on her ankle.

"While Miss Dibben was away, the minister's wife, Mrs. Prosser, and her two little boys came over and stayed with me. She was a very jolly person and it was nice of her to come just before Christmas. Unfortunately, Miss Dibben hadn't finished making our grocery list, and as the groceries came up once a week from Minstrel Island, we had run out of nearly everything. We had prayers one night and Mrs. Prosser said, 'Everyone has to go home. I wish you could stay, but we have no coal-oil, and we can't have tea because we've run out of tea.' The people looked at us so strangely, and the next night everyone came with bottles of preserves and coal-oil and tea to tide us over. This was a small village and everyone knew everyone, and we were all friendly together.

Oscar Soderman's camp in Knight Inlet, a typical floating village.

Floating homes at Echo Bay, 1926.

"It was very stormy that year, and it rained so much. A storm blew our clothesline down, which went from the float across the bay to a tree. On the day that Miss Dibben broke her ankle, we returned from Alert Bay. It was wild and stormy and there was Mrs. Prosser at the end of the wharf trying to pull in the washing. The line broke and all the washing went in the water. The tide went in and out and there was muddy silt all over everything. We had to wash all over again and used various clotheslines up and down the village.

"It's rather nice to be in a village where the people are all Indian people. They didn't consider us to be 'white people.' We were part of the village. I remember a Christmas concert and party. Adults came as well as children, and people brought food. We played Indian games. I remember they had a broom and someone would point it and try to make another person laugh. If they made someone laugh, that was a point for them. We had a really good time. I never got home for Christmas as transportation was too difficult.

"You get very nosy when you live in an isolated place. You hear a fishboat coming from a long way off and everyone goes down to see who it is. When they come ashore, you ask what they came for, who they are, and how long they are going to stay. You have to know everything! I suppose it's because people don't have enough social contacts. The children knew their fathers' boats long before they came in sight by the sound of the engines.

"The long houses in the village were still in use at that time. One winter they had a really large potlatch. Someone wrote Ottawa and reported it, so the Mounties came to Village Island. People had come from Fort Rupert and Turner Island, and they were all in our house when the Mounties came because we had prayers at night. The Indian agent was

Students at Echo Bay School, 1926. L to R: Arnold Rose, Mildred Rose, Gail McCay, unidentified. Second row: Leonard Rose, Irene Rose, Ione McCay.

quite angry too. He told everyone to go home, but they wouldn't. They said if they stopped the potlatch, they would have to start all over again.

"It was the celebration of the Hommetza. There were two of these 'Wild Men' and they stayed in the woods with attendants, living off the land until enticed back to the village.

"At night everyone sat around the sides of the long house. There was a huge fire in the middle. There were all kinds of dances with bird and animal masks and cedar bark costumes, and they did all kinds of magic things. Someone rose from the ground and his hat went all around him and came back on his head, and there was eagle down floating all over. But you know, it's in the dark with only the light from the fire in the centre. How do they do it? I don't know.

"Finally the Wild Men came down through a hole in the roof, and did a wild kind of dance around the fire, and went out again.

"The potlatch went on for several days. The Mounties were all tall and overwhelming, but the chief was taller, and had a high hat on, and was speaking Indian. The Mounties didn't understand what was going on and, of course, they never saw anyone give anything away at the potlatch.

"Miss Dibben didn't attend, but she said it was alright for me to go. She didn't judge one way or the other whether it was right or wrong. I myself haven't any idea why they banned the potlatch. It's very difficult for older people to change from the old way of life. The potlatch looked after all the old people when they couldn't fish anymore. They received back what they had given, and it was their due. As soon as they weren't allowed to have the potlatch anymore, it was chaotic.

"While the potlatch was going on, there were a lot of children in school. They came

Smaller float camps hired teachers on a private tutor basis to oversee correspondence lessons.

pouring in from all those villages, and they all went to school. I'd have thirty or more instead of the usual six or seven, and some had never been to school before. Every single person would be in a different grade, and there wasn't material or books! Besides this, the Wild Men in the woods were getting bored. They would come near the school and call out their cannibal cry and try to scare the children.

"Some people told me that the Wild Men saw me going through the woods one day. I went along a trail to get milk and eggs from a farm in the next bay, and the dog knew they were there because he chased them. The people said the Wild Men surely ran because if we had met, they would have had to chase me and take a bite!

"I taught at Village Island four years. It certainly was more interesting than lots of places, but there wasn't any social life for a girl. It was lonely sometimes, especially at Christmas.

"I remember my first look at the village. It was so traumatic. A lady in an Indian canoe was coming into the bay. She was wailing and grieving and crying out because she had just lost her son.

"It was a spooky place at night because the totem poles were unpainted, and had weathered a lovely silvery colour. There was one pointing sternly, and Mrs. Prosser said it was the first schoolteacher.

"All this happened a long time ago. This year, I went back to the Centennial of the Alert Bay Anglican Church. I met many of my former pupils who had moved to Alert Bay, Port Hardy, and Port McNeill. There is no one living on Village Island anymore. It is a beautiful place but now that it is abandoned to the weeds and trees, it must be quite mournful and sad."

The Teachers Remember

Ask a former teacher to talk about early days, and a flood of memories is apt to be released, carrying with it a great mixture of pleasure, pain, and amusement. Although life may have taken many turns since teaching days, these early impressions remain sharp and clear.

"The loneliness was just awful," says Ellwood Rice, and with these words he takes us back over the years to two small settlements in Central B.C.: a place called Salmon River, which waited in vain for the PGE to come through, and a railway siding called Hulatt, about seventeen miles from Vanderhoof.

"To get there in winter in those days, you had to travel four or five hours by snowshoe. The first thing the inspector of schools said when he dropped me off that day was, 'You'd better get a pair of snowshoes.' I said, 'That school sits pretty high there,' and he said, 'In the winter, you'll know why.'

"At both my schools, I stayed in a teacherage. This had some advantages over boarding because there is always friction over who is going to board the teacher, because of the money. These were tough times so money was very important.

"We got mail every two weeks. We had to walk down to what we called the post-office, four miles downhill on the Salmon River. There was a little library there, and you could take out a few books to pass away the time, but there was no place to visit. You were entirely alone, except for the children in the school. There were no young people your own age, just a load of bachelors, old homesteaders, and three families. One boy of seven walked four miles to school. It would be dark when he got home—bushed in right along the road, and no houses along the way.

"I've seen the time there when I'd get up in the middle of the night and play my phonograph. I'd be almost frantic with the feeling of things closing in and the silence. I suppose if you'd grown up in that kind of country, there'd be no problem. But to have grown up in the city and to go there . . . looking back, it was a wonderful experience, but it gave me grey hair pretty young.

"There was nothing to do on the weekend. I went hunting one day and got thoroughly lost for a day and a half under sub-zero conditions. I thought I'd go out after school just to get away from things. After a long time, I looked at my snowshoe tracks with a flashlight. I thought, 'Gosh, I'm on my own tracks again.' They got me out of there, just by chance, the next day.

"The Salmon River School was well constructed. It had a teacherage which was, I suppose, ten-by-twenty, and had two rooms. Right behind the teacher's desk in the school was a door going into the kitchen, and the teacher could have his meal cooking while teaching. The children used to say, 'This is beans day.' I was a bachelor and had never cooked before. The weak oil lamps were the only lighting. I have poor eyesight, and I don't know how I managed, as I used to read every night before I fell asleep. Water was hauled four miles to the school. Someone had a contract to bring it in.

Teacher Pauline Romaine and friend about to set up shop in Brilliant, 1932.

"This was a young person's country, there was no doubt about that. It went down to sixty-five degrees below zero (fahrenheit). One way you knew was that you could hear the trees splitting and the spikes pulling on the railway platforms. In the summer the mosquitoes were very bad. Sometimes you couldn't see the sky for the clouds of them. Then, after the mosquitoes, the black flies came.

"Salmon River was built up because of the hope that the railway would come through some day—the old PGE. The people had been sold the property while they were on the prairies with the idea that the country was going to boom. Life for them was unbelievably tough.

"We had no Christmas concert because there was longstanding tension between the people who lived there. However, I did spend Christmas with a Scandinavian family, and that was interesting. People dropped in for dinner. There were some trappers who talked mostly Norwegian, but I could understand the odd word, and at least I was with people.

"My next school was at Hulatt, a section and tie-hacking town about seventeen miles from Vanderhoof. It had a store and a post-office.

"The inspector of schools had come to me and said that there were problems there, and would I take the school?

"In the first place, there were two school boards, each one claiming to be the legal one. Then, among the children, there was a ring-leader who had come from Vancouver. To keep him from going to jail the judge had

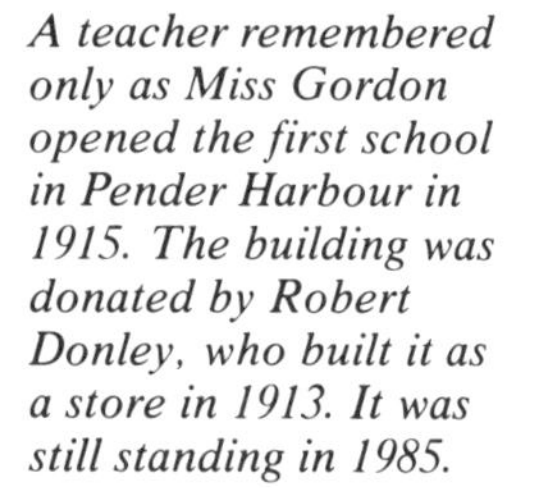

A teacher remembered only as Miss Gordon opened the first school in Pender Harbour in 1915. The building was donated by Robert Donley, who built it as a store in 1913. It was still standing in 1985.

said, 'Get him out into the hinterland, and let him go free.' He gathered a gang of five or six of the older boys, and they broke into boxcars, got into the theatre and ran behind the screen, and broke horses loose.

"The inspector asked me if I would take on this school because the police said the boys would be sent to reform school unless someone could handle them. The school had been closed because of it.

"When I first went to this school, I knew it was a tough situation so, for the first two weeks, I was a martinet. I had to let them know who was boss. Somebody told me when I went there, 'We come from various European countries. There's a saying there, "When the King is in the land, things go well," so be the King.'

"After a few weeks I eased up, and we had about the friendliest, least formal school in the province. We learned to respect one another, and they learned self-discipline. The independent spirit and energy of those boys was channelled. They could so easily have gone down the wrong road at that time.

"Our Governor-General said today on the radio, 'Well, I grew up going to a one-room school, and then I went to University, and later became Premier of Manitoba.' Teachers have a tremendous challenge to inspire children to things beyond the course of study.

"Living conditions weren't too good in Hulatt. I was just married, and my wife and I slept on a cot under the staircase in the waiting room of the section-house. There was a teacherage of sorts, a little log cabin behind the school, but you could see daylight through the walls. We chinked it up by mixing manure with clay so the wind didn't blow through, and we furnished it after a fashion, and at last we were on our own. We got our water from the Nechako River and chopped ice in the winter.

"The country was cold. You could hear the spikes pulling like rifle shots. I recall a dance at Meadowdale. When we got there, we just had to walk the horses around all night or they would have frozen to death. You associated coldness with that country.

"The kind of drink they had up there was pretty rough stuff. I remember I went up to the police and applied for an excise permit to make beer. He said, 'Go on and make it, everyone here does.' I said, 'Mr. Jennens, if someone wanted to report me, you would have to prosecute me, and that wouldn't be good for the school system here. I'm going to put you to all the bother of coming up to inspect it.' I still have the excise permit today. When I left that country I didn't have one single drink for years, yet we drank there every day of the year. There was always somebody coming in to say 'Hello' and you'd have a drink with them.

"There's no purpose for Hulatt to exist any more. There are no more ties to be cut, and the railways have fewer section-houses. The buildings are falling down now. Life was good in those days, if you could cope with it."

A teacher in the village of Telegraph Creek on the Stikine River in the 1940s may have experienced some loneliness, but the haunting and romantic atmosphere of that area made up for any hardship:

"Over thirty-five years have passed since I taught school in Telegraph Creek, yet I still return there in my mind, wandering around the village as though nothing has changed.

"In my memory it's usually springtime, the hills covered with wild roses and blue polymonium, the river running free of ice, and the sun shining. I see the little settlement scattered above the brown, swirling Stikine River, a few tin roofs shining, and a flag flying in front of the Hudson's Bay store.

"Down the hills hurry familiar figures, some of them the school children, for the first boat in the spring is coming up the river, whistle blowing and engine throbbing. She is carrying freight, groceries, mail, and a bottle or two. Above all, there are visitors with news of the 'outside.'

"Amid the pandemonium the captain, Al Ritchie, steps ashore carrying a box of oranges for the children. He hoists the box up the hill on his shoulder, and all the kids run behind.

"It was not my idea to teach in Telegraph Creek. In May of 1946 I left Vancouver for Wrangell, Alaska, on a CPR boat. I then transferred to a river boat, the *Judith Ann*, to go to the Diamond B big-game ranch on the Stikine River, for I had a job as a cook's helper for the summer. I planned to go the twelve miles up river to Telegraph Creek in late September, just to have a look at the old town before returning to civilization. Fate intervened, however, in the person of Miss Nancy Dunn.

"Among the people who met the boat that September was a tall, white-haired woman with very blue eyes and an English accent. She was the sole nurse in charge of the outpost hospital, and also the school trustee. Miss Dunn approached me at once, and with a voice that sounded like the British Empire, she told me that God must have sent me to Telegraph Creek. The school was without a teacher and she had heard that I was a teacher. My duty was plain, for I looked up at the bank and saw a bewildering number of children's faces, dark and lively.

"I faced up to Miss Dunn really well. I told her I was certainly leaving on the boat the next day. That night she came to see me, and I stayed. I've been grateful to Miss Dunn ever since.

"The little town probably numbered about three hundred people in those days, most of them Tahltan Indians. They are tall, handsome people whose blood was sometimes mixed with early explorers, trappers, and adventurers. Their trapping and hunting areas were so vast they seemed like kingdoms. Fur prices were good and they traded beaver, mink, marten, wolverine, and fox skins to the Hudson's Bay or independent traders. Big-game hunters hired Tahltan guides, for that country was famous for Stone and Dall sheep, goats, cariboo, and grizzly bear.

Opposite: *Telegraph Creek.*

"Looking back, I picture we outsiders—the government agent, Indian agent, nurse, teacher, telegraph operator, Catholic priest, Anglican minister, Hudson's Bay manager, and policeman—as rather jumpy souls, not quite at ease in that wilderness. I believe the character of those who stayed long enough gradually weathered like the older inhabitants and the town itself.

"There were several other settlements close by. Dry Town, with its old patched log houses, stretched along the high bank above the river, and Black Casca was reached by a steep trail. The Bear Lake Indians lived across the river and you could hear their dogs howling at night, answering the dogs of Dry Town. People used dogs in those days—dog teams when the ice was on the river, and pack dogs in the summer. There was only one vehicle in Telegraph Creek, an ancient truck that made trips over the steep tortuous road to Dease Lake.

"Spread out peacefully above the river were two stores, a few government buildings, and the houses with their little gardens of vegetables and old-fashioned flowers.

"The school was perched above the town, next to the outpost hospital. It was a two-storey building of white-washed logs, built about the turn of the century. The carved head of a bear in the graveyard above loomed over the bank, and from the school you could hear the creek as it rushed down the hill, cutting through the town.

"The teacher always lived above the school, reaching the two rooms by a rickety flight of steps. I was quite taken aback when I saw the furnishings—some boxes, an old chair and table, a sagging bed in the back room, two coal-oil lamps, a Yukon heater, and a wretched cook stove that smoked.

"One of the school boys brought water from a flume, charging by the pail. The method looked Chinese—a long pole balanced on the shoulder with a pail at each end. Several Chinese had settled in Telegraph Creek after the gold rush.

"Along one wall of the teacherage were storage bins. These were meant for flour and

Question: Where is the teacher in this 1946 Telegraph Creek School picture? Answer: Far left, second row.

sugar, but if the teacher was smart they would also be full of potatoes, carrots, and onions, for after the boat stopped running, vegetables were scarce. I was improvident and the mice ran freely up and down the bins all winter. By spring I was eating canned butter, powdered eggs, hard tack, and cans of beans and peaches. Heinz catsup made all these miserable meals taste the same. I was always so grateful if someone gave me a piece of moose meat.

"There were fifty-five children on the school register that year. They were really patient with me on the first day, explaining which were Indian and which white. Payment was made by both governments in proportion to these statistics.

"Attendance fluctuated wildly, due to trapping, epidemics of flu, woodcutting, fishing at Tahltan, potato planting, and so on. It was such a hardship for some of the older boys to attend school in the spring. I remember a teen-age boy pleading to be allowed to go on the beaver hunt. The trouble was that in those days the family allowance would have been withheld.

"Our school received little attention from the outside world, and none from the inspector of schools. Sometimes the stove pipes separated, causing the roof to catch on fire. The desks were held together with strips of babiche, maps were tattered and ancient, and there were no books but the readers. The sole decoration was a tin Dewar's Whiskey calendar, the kind that will go on forever.

"Despite this initial starkness, our school became a cheerful place. We had home-made checkers and cards, and a wind-up gramophone and guitar. We departed often from the course of studies, . . . and we made reasons to go outside. We studied birds, flowers, seeds, insects, and snow flakes.

"One fall afternoon the children and I heard a jingling clattering sound. We rushed outside for they knew what it was. Down the hill came a long Hudson's Bay pack train laden with the horns and heads of mountain goat and cariboo.

"Our school trustee, Miss Dunn, was a colourful person. Dressed for one of her official trips by dog team to some small settlement, she was very dramatic with a tall fur hat, parka trimmed with wolverine, high beaded mukluks, and huge cariboo-hide gloves trimmed with velvet and beads.

"It was Miss Dunn's idea to start a youth club. One frosty night we had a treasure hunt, with clues laid from Ah Clem's to the graveyard. The sound of young people running all over town in the dark made the police nervous.

"Christmas in Telegraph Creek was a great occasion. All the trappers came home and, besides the concert, there were dances in the hall and plenty of home-brew. Putting on a dance was easy—two gas lamps, two fiddlers, and moccasin telegraph did the rest.

"They danced the old square dances, but some time during the night the fiddlers were sure to play, 'Take Me Back to Telegraph, I'm Too Young to Marry.' They played very fast while the dancers did some strange step called the 'Telegraph Creek Hop.'

"Speaking of home-brew, people wore metal 'creepers' over their moccasins and rubbers in winter, to help them climb the slippery hills. It was said that on some nights, there were people who needed them on their mitts as well.

"Newcomers often contracted cabin fever by spring, so very strange things happened before the ice broke on the river. I was very surprised to receive a summons from the policeman which suggested that I was bringing liquor up to the reserve. The incensed government agent urged me to sue him, an interesting suggestion to relieve the winter monotony. I became confused and consequently did nothing. One night as I was doing school work, there was a bang on the door. It was the policeman, asking in aggrieved tones why I had not obeyed his summons. Someone, he stated, had seen me carrying a bottle up to Black Casca the night of a birthday dance. It took time to convince him that I had snowshoed up there with the Hudson's Bay clerk, carrying only a box of cigars. Over coffee we both agreed that the winter is long and one can get bushed by spring.

"Life has changed in Telegraph Creek. There is a road to the Alaska Highway, and another south to Hazelton, so that the river boats no longer run. A decline in fur prices, inroads of mining exploration, and an influx of white homesteaders—all this has changed the Telegraph Creek that I remember.

"I prefer not to think of snowmobiles, helicopters, tourists, and heavy equipment, but to keep my own memories—the mournful sound of sled dogs howling, fiddle music floating across lonesome Dease Lake, and the fast-flowing, ever-changing Stikine River. Above all, I remember the boys and girls of Telegraph Creek. They are entwined in my memory with their wild and beautiful surroundings."

Early in January 1928 another young woman set out for a teaching position in a country school not far from Burns Lake. Schools were hard to get then, and teachers took any positions they could find. She suffered a great deal, but as her story shows, she was brave and resourceful.

"Once on the northern line, the way seemed endless . . . miles and miles of wooded country, here and there a lonely section-house, a small homestead, or a trapper's cabin, and one or two larger settlements such as Prince George —at that time still very much a pioneer town.

"The trainmen knew all the teachers up and down the line, and the conditions of the places where they taught. In fact everyone seemed to know everyone in that country.

"Of course they learned where I was headed, and I sensed a few eyebrows raised. Nothing was said.

"I reached the station where I was to leave the train, just after midnight. A flag stop only. It was twelve below zero. I got off one end of the train into a snow drift, and my trunk was put off ahead onto the station platform. The only building was the unlit station, and no lights anywhere to be seen. I stood watching the two red eyes of the retreating train, knowing there would not be another for three days.

"Then far up the hill above me, I saw a tiny wavering light, and all I could do was wait.

"After what seemed ages, an old man with a lantern arrived. He said he was to take me to the hotel, and that the school secretary would be in, in the morning, to take me out to the settlement where I was to teach.

"We dragged my trunk into the empty station, and toiled up the narrow trail by lantern light to the settlement above. We came to a small house.

"There were no electric lights or other amenities. We entered a sitting room . . . no sign of this being a hotel . . . no register or anything of that sort. I was shown through a curtained door into a large bedroom with two beds, and told to take whichever I liked. I was given an oil lamp and matches.

"The old man went off and, tired as I was

after three day's travel, I waited until all the lights were off, and no signs of movement anywhere, then crawled into the nearest bed. All was spotlessly clean.

"Sunday morning I awoke to hear men's voices beyond the wavy curtain, and wondered where I had landed. I finally held a blanket ahead of me, hung it over the string which held the wavy curtain, and got dressed.

"I went out timidly, to be greeted by the wife of the old man who had conducted me up from the train. She was a dear, and they were the proprietors of the hotel.

"I was mothered and fed, and received nothing but kindness. Later, when I knew this old couple better, they were dear friends and did much for me through the years that I knew them.

"At noon, two men arrived to drive me out to the place where I was to teach.

"We started out by team and bob-sleigh, down the hill to the station, where my trunk was loaded on. Then we went southward, across the ice of the frozen river into the wilds. It was a rough trail, through what seemed like endless woods, dodging stumps here and there.

"The men would get off the sleigh and walk at times, to keep warm, and I would have done so, but each time I suggested it, they said we were nearly at our destination. I got colder and colder.

"At last, about midnight, we arrived at a small house where we dropped off the mail, then another mile through the woods until we came to the log house of the secretary, where I was to board.

"I was given no choice, and found later that it was the only house in the district with more than one room.

"And what a room it was! Just partitioned off from the main living room, or kitchen, by lathes and brown paper reaching to just above my head. There was no ceiling, but a rickety door. The bed springs had a hole in the middle and sagged almost to the floor. A rickety dresser, a shelf with an enamel basin, and my trunk, were the sole furnishings.

"This family was living on a stump farm. They did some trapping, but their chief income was the teacher's board money which was $35 a month. (In those days this was considered high.)

"There were no comforts. I had to get my own water... drinking water from a creek, melted snow for washing. In spring a small lake flooded a plowed field, and one put on waders and, taking a dipper and bucket, ladled the water from the furrows, and strained out the polliwogs through a large handkerchief.

"Monday morning I found my way up to the school... a mile up a trail through the woods.

"The children were unsophisticated and had seen little of civilization, beyond a tiny village. I had children from three families. They all came on foot through the wooded trails.

"One family did a bit of trapping along the way. On my first day at school, a six-year-old youngster approached me holding a weasel up by the tail. He asked me how much he should get for it. I did not know the value of furs, but found later he would get 25¢ for it. It would be sent away with his father's furs.

"Of course in winter, all wore boy's rubbers and heavy socks. But when it got warmer, some came barefoot. One very poor family would carry their shoes, and put them on just before approaching the school.

"There was a very fine Swedish family, two girls and a small boy, who walked four-and-a-half miles from a lonely canyon on the river. In winter they put extra socks over their rubbers to keep them from slipping. They only missed one day of school, when it was fifty-nine below zero, but turned up the next day at fifty-five below, the only pupils to do so.

"Conditions in the district were not good. Nearly all the families were quarrelling with one another, and all 'agin the law.' Anyone who represented the 'law' was practically anathema. Of course they tried to involve the teacher, who had to be very close-mouthed and not take sides.

"They tried to run the school for me, until it got to the point where I was almost desperate, sticking very close to the school law, by the letter. I appealed to the inspector, not realizing my letters were being intercepted.

"Finally one of the Mounted Police came out to the district. A certain party had accused Indians of stealing beaver off his trapline, while in reality it was the other way around. The stolen beaver was hanging under a large trap-door where I was boarding, and later we ate it.

"The Mounted Police came up to the school, and I told him my difficulties. It was at least someone from the outside whom I could talk to. I asked him to contact the inspector and also to stop my mail at the source.

"That meant I could no longer post or get

Remote Cariboo ranch, 1919. Families in such areas often competed to board the teacher, and the board money was sometimes their largest source of income.

mail without a fifteen-mile walk over the bush trail each weekend . . . but it was worth it.

"I would often be six or eight hours on the way through the bush, sometimes breaking trail through the snow. Occasionally I could get a horse, but usually I was on foot. I would go off early Saturday morning with a light pack. I always carried a chocolate bar or two, a pocket knife, matches, in case I had to camp along the way. But that was never necessary. I stayed with friends in the settlement, left clothes there, and hiked out again on the Sunday afternoon.

"Though often hard, I got to enjoy that trail, the woods were so beautiful. I often saw moose and bear. Birds, squirrels, and chipmunks were everywhere. One night after dark, coming around a bend, I came across a tiny campfire. An old Indian was cooking a fish on the end of a stick. We chatted for a few minutes. He would probably spend the night there. It was most unusual to come across anyone on my way.

"On this week-end journey to pick up the mail, I had to cross quite a large river. A cable ferry, propelled by the current, would carry passengers or wagons. When the river was frozen, the ferry was taken out, and one walked across on the ice.

"In early spring there would be stretches of mud and long puddles. One would try to crawl along logs at the side of the trail to bypass these stretches. In winter often it would be snowing and one would have to break the trail.

"The year was full of hardships and I knew I could not stand it much longer. I would clean the school, and stay working up there until dark, but as there were no lights I would have to leave. Then, at the house, I could not use my bedroom, but had to spread my books on the end of the table in the main room, and work while the man of the house skinned his beaver and muskrat at the other end of the table. The skins were stretched and hung around the log walls, and the carcasses thrown out through the door. You can imagine the flies in the spring.

"There was practically no conversation, as I dared not open my mouth, but listened to the shortcomings of all my predecessors and others in the district.

"The food was very poor, an occasional deer but mostly moose meat. Moose meat and fried potatoes for breakfast, moose meat sandwiches for lunch, and moose meat and fried potatoes for supper, with perhaps a fruit or cake.

"For six weeks the cows were dry and we had no butter. That meant dry sandwiches of moose meat.

"When the cows were milking again, we had a wad of butter on the table, but you had to dodge the black hairs. If a pudding was made, the bowl was put on the floor for the small child to lick out. . . and reused without washing.

"About half a mile from where I lived was an elderly couple with no children. They had a square log house with one room only, but it was spotless. I used to often wander up there in the evenings, just to get away from my boarding place, and they were very good to me.

"I told them that I could no longer stand the place where I was staying, and that I was leaving, and so they built a little log cabin alongside their house for me. The cabin was simple. They gathered moss and chinked between the logs, and put in a good air-tight heater. It was cozy, and there I stayed until I went to another school further west.

"Of course moving from my former place caused trouble, as the whole family were practically living on my board money. They raved about my going and I had quite a time getting out. I took what I could out by hand, but another family with several big boys rescued my trunk out by the bedroom window.

"I was in that district a year and a half, and held the record for time there as a teacher. The next year they sent in a man teacher, and after that the school closed."

Teacher Don Smith.

Don Smith began his first year of teaching in 1936 at a small settlement in the Peace River country. Large numbers of homesteaders had arrived in that area after the Hart Highway and the railway made it accessible to the south of the province. It was a tough land. Farms were far apart, the summers were short, and the winter temperatures dipped as low as eighty degrees below zero (fahrenheit).

The depression severely affected life in the Peace River. In the area where Don Smith taught, the staple diet was moose meat and little else. He learned how basic living conditions can be. He was young and enthusiastic and enjoyed the experience.

"I travelled from Vancouver to Edmonton, and then to Dawson Creek by bus, and then by horse and buggy, and finally arrived at a very small settlement with a very small one-room school.

"I found I was to live with a family—father, mother, and six children, with myself making nine altogether. They were fine people, close to nature, living frugally, and very kind-hearted.

"The school itself was a small, log, one-room building—the student population being ten. I didn't have to enroll anyone to keep the roll up to eight. Ten youngsters, eight grades, and a greenhorn teacher.

"The settlement was small and congenial. The teacher was looked upon as someone to help in all regards, even outside the teaching category.

"Most difficult was adjusting to country living. The climate was different. On the fourteenth of September, it snowed four feet. This closed the school for a week and was a rude initiation. However, I was raised on the prairies and so survived the first snowstorm.

"Our only source of entertainment was the occasional schoolhouse dance. We began at nine and went until midnight, then we had dinner, continued on to three in the morning when we had a lunch, and finished at six in the morning. The children came, and as the hour grew later, each child was wrapped up and put under a desk, and there they remained until the break-up of the dance when they were taken home to sleep most of the next day, along with their parents and a tired schoolteacher. These dances were the social highlight of the community, and although vigorous, they were most enjoyable.

"That first year was a bit of a trial. At Normal I learned a fair amount, but how much would apply in a one-room school with eight grades was another matter. It was like running a three-ring circus; however, it was a wonderful way to learn the job from the ground up.

"For the two years that I remained in that community, I did not taste any tame meat. We lived entirely off the land. I found it most nourishing, and I put on a little weight, something I had not done for a long time. I adjusted to the routine of meals. Moose was plentiful—moose steak with black, sugarless coffee for breakfast; lunch was two baking powder biscuits with a wedge of moose meat between and no butter; dinner was moose with possibly potatoes and a large quantity of white beans, again accompanied by black, sugarless coffee—not a very interesting diet, but substantial. Part of the success was the fact that the chap I lived with had an amazing way of curing the meat. Different parts were cured differently, and although we had it three times a day, it never tasted the same. This made it bearable and I enjoyed it.

"The people in that community did a little hunting and trapping, but not much farming. The income of the people I lived with consisted mostly of the board I paid them—twenty-five dollars a month—plus a small income from the post office. Their needs were not great. The man of the house would get a little money together and make the three-day trip to Dawson Creek. He would buy a few essentials—sugar, flour, ammunition, beans, and one or two other items. The other sources of food were hunting and the garden, which helped make a balanced diet.

"We had central heating in the school—one big barrel stove with a stovepipe going out the roof. It was the job of the teacher to arrive early enough to heat the school and to light the lamps in winter (it was dark at nine o'clock and again at two o'clock in the afternoon), and to bring in some ice for drinking water. I made some attempt at the close of school each day to clean the building. There was no pay for it.

"We had a blackboard, a box of chalk, and a few books. There were readers but students had to share. Supplies were meagre but students had pencils and paper.

"This is one of the calamities I ran into at my first school. At night, we put papers and pencils in the desks; as each child only had one pencil, and town was far away, it was a matter of making sure that pencils didn't get lost. This was good training in itself.

"Pencils began to disappear and no one was prepared to point the finger at anyone else.

Don Smith (left).

"The school itself was a small, log, one room building . . ." Don Smith.

After one weekend, we returned to the school on Monday to find almost half the students were without pencils. It became evident that something was amiss.

"I related the problem to the man at my boarding place. He said, 'Don, I know what your problem is. You have a four-legged pack rat in the school. If you let me come down, I can find him.' Back we went that same evening, and into the attic of the log school, and we found the pencils in a neat pile, and other missing items. We sealed up the hole in the attic and that solved the mystery of the missing pencils!

"After two years, I moved to another community seven miles north of Dawson Creek, again a one-room school but a very different community.

"I went from the boarding place I first described to one almost the complete opposite. I moved in with a Swedish gentleman with a wife that was Danish. From a diet of moose meat and beans to Danish pastry! It was a shock to the system.

"I was happy in this new situation. It was not as basic a community. The people were interested in their children but were also interested in the running of the school. The parents were cooperative and willing to help, but the community had its differences, some irritating and some amusing.

Opposite: *School picnic in the Okanagan, 1922.*

"I will quote from a letter received from a parent who was a constant correspondent. This gives some idea of what might be involved:

> Dear Mr. Smith,
>
> Please do not be hurt or offended. There are things no one can help. You have been so kind and good to Bunny.
>
> Anyone might swear, but I wish you would please curb vulgar and immodest talk. Mrs. L. was boiling mad at the things that boy told her boy. He's tough but he don't get a square deal at home, for I give him my sympathy. Can you please see that things run smooth and don't let them talk of such things?
>
> Mrs. S. has done her stuff that I resent. When her daughter told my daughter to clean her fingernails, I told Bunny to tell her to mind her own business. Her husband is nice and we enjoy his company, but we resent interference. Homestead life is enough in itself.
>
> As long as Bunny likes you, you are welcome to anything we can give you and will be your friend for life.

"One of the highlights of the experience in the Peace River was the annual Teachers' Convention. All people who attended were one-room schoolteachers who gathered together and tried to solve their problems and have a good social time. We did not see our colleagues other than at these conventions or on the trip in and out of the country.

"The four years in the one-room school were a real experience, and looking back, I don't think I would have done otherwise because these four years taught me more about the art of teaching than anything I learned at Normal School, or anything I learned afterwards. It was a basis which was a boon to me in later teaching years, and an experience which I really look back on.

"I went on to be involved in graded schools and in the administration of schools. I feel the one-room school gave a very sound education. We did lack many things, but the teaching of the three Rs was soundly done. It taught youngsters to be independent while helping others. This is something one can not find anywhere else but in the one-room school, and for this reason I believe they made a great contribution."

The Pupils Remember

A reunion of one-room school pupils is bound to be an emotional event. With enthusiastic cries of recognition, pupils who have not seen each other for thirty, forty, fifty, or sixty years greet each other and nostalgically recall the old school, all the hardships and poverty of equipment, the lessons they learned, and the adventures along the trail to the schoolhouse. Invariably, the conversation turns to three topics: "teachers we had," "games we played at recess," and "pranks we played on the teacher."

Such a school reunion was held in July 1981, at Meldrum Creek in the Chilcotin. The school opened in 1914 with twelve pupils, and closed in 1969 with nine pupils. During those years it housed a total of thirty-four teachers and some five hundred pupils. Over two hundred of these former students and their teachers travelled to the reunion, held at the site of the original log school which still stands on property that belonged to Thomas Meldrum.

Under the trees by the dilapidated log school, guests enjoyed a picnic lunch, played horseshoes, and danced to old-time tunes. Of course everyone brought snapshots and photograph albums, and many were the stories told by the pupils of Meldrum Creek School.

Ruth Barrs, one of the teachers who attended the reunion, was recalled affectionately by former pupils as being a very naive girl. It seems they had taken her on a "snipe hunt" in a swampy area where she was left with a sack and a lantern. The pupils, who were supposed to chase the snipe in her direction, then went home to play cards. Some time later, they saw a little light coming across the fields—their unfortunate teacher returning from the snipe hunt. It was recalled also that Miss Barrs had a pond named after her. "Schoolmarm Pond" received its name when a horse took a notion to roll while Miss Barrs was still on its back.

Attempts are often made by old-timers, the historians of their area, to recall the seemingly endless succession of one-room schoolteachers who came and went over the years. Some are remembered only by name, while others are vividly recalled for their idiosyncrasies or their outstanding abilities. Ed Zscheidrich, who attended Dragon Lake School near Quesnel, recalls such a long list of schoolmarms and schoolmasters that, as he says, "The whole place would be peppered with teachers if they all got married and settled here.

"There was Miss Robinson; she was the first teacher that opened the school in 1913. Then there was Miss McLougtin the following year, but she resigned at Christmas time. They made it so miserable for her that she had to resign. Then there was a fellow, David

Class at the Maple Leaf School, Pender Harbour.

School at the Cameron family ranch house, 1914.

McQueen; he took her place at Christmas-on, but he disappeared and never came back. Then there was Sykes for a term, and then there was a man named Beal—he was a timid sheep. Then this Ellis guy, and Miss Driver, and Miss Champion . . ."

and so on, through the whole ghostly list of saints, eccentrics, alcoholics, and inspired teachers, some of whom became legends, long discussed and chuckled over.

Of course most often talked about were the oddities and misfits. Macalister School in the Cariboo had its full share of these. One former pupil remembers a teacher so terrible that he taught the same things to all eight grades. "He had one lesson and that was it. If you happened to be in Grade One, too bad! If you happened to be in Grade Eight, too bad!" This teacher covered his deficiencies by giving all pupils straight "A"s on their report cards. Another teacher at this same school had been a surveyor and probably should have stuck to his trade. He alarmed the parents of his star pupil by giving him a "special demerit."

The unfortunate Mr. Sykes who taught at Dragon Lake School crops up again at Macalister School, and his disgraceful conduct lives on in the memories of James Macalister, one of his pupils:

"I don't know how they got hold of Sykes. He was hired during the Great War when you couldn't get teachers. He liked to drink, and he got fired because he got drunk down at the school. Prohibition had just started and he thought he'd better stock up while he could still buy it. He was able to walk the half mile down to the school and tell us kids to go home, but he got himself stuck in the mud down there. We kids told on him and he got fired."

Among the other eccentrics who taught at Macalister was an elderly lady who sat by the stove, keeping herself warm and leaving the children to freeze. This lady had seen better days and chose to wear out all her old-fashioned finery at the school. In the majesty of long evening dresses, she looked quite incongruous in the tiny school room.

Charles Henderson, who attended the Commonage School near Vernon, remembers a young lady teacher who hadn't quite accepted the responsibility of her position. Instead, she saddled him with it.

"Our teacher had a boyfriend in Kelowna, and every weekend she used to go there to visit him. On Mondays she was always tired and so she used to ask me to teach the others while she curled up and slept in the cloakroom. I had strict orders to wake her up if I saw anyone coming."

And so the parade passed by. Although pupils might remember a teacher who became bushed and hid under the bed, or another with such a broad Scots accent that no one could understand a word he said, most fondly remembered were the fair, strict disciplinarians who would stand for no nonsense, and the teachers who inspired, taught, and loved their pupils. It was all a matter of style, for with only a dozen or so unsophisticated children to observe, a one-room schoolteacher was in control of a little kingdom. Thus, long afterwards, pupils could compare and recall the styles of various teachers—the sergeant majors, the dramatic actors, the pedantic and exacting, the hearty outdoor types, the warm and friendly ones, and the timid who could be harassed beyond their limits.

The pupils of one Cariboo school tried out every new teacher by rolling huge boulders down the great rock hill behind the school. Some teachers nipped this practice in the bud right away, but one was not firm enough. Eventually, an enormous boulder crashed right through the wall of the school.

In the spring, water poured down this same hill, and the children patiently routed the water into the schoolyard, creating a sea of mud between the school and the teacherage. The teacher put planks across. This was perfect, for the students then removed the planks, leaving the teacher marooned in the knee-deep mud.

Teacher-baiting didn't always work, and sometimes a teacher had the last laugh. Kathy Yorston remembers a bright sunny morning in March when one teacher started off to school on the rather tired old horse of which she was quite proud. Some school children, wishing to show her that her horse was a slow old plug, took off their shoes, stowed them under a bridge, and sprinted past her on the trail, arriving at school long ahead of her. Although annoyed by the triumphant smiles of the children, the teacher said nothing. Toward afternoon, the temperature dropped and it began to snow. There was no help from the teacher, so after school the children faced a nightmare of running through crusted snow with bare feet. First they stopped to light an old rat's nest, then took shelter in a pigsty where they lit the straw, and finally scurried to the shelter of a culvert. At last, with numb and bleeding feet, they put on their shoes and reached home, "pretty mad" at the teacher, but realizing they had it coming to them.

On the subject of "teacher harassment,"

something should be said about the almost forgotten slate pencil. Arthur Peake tells us that at Athalmer School there were two varieties of slate pencil:

"One was a soft pencil, not too unpleasant or too hard on the ears of the sensitive members of the class, and the other was cheaper and sharper and squealed to high heaven when you wrote anything on the slate. The latter was favoured because if you held it the right way, it would screech loudly enough to send everyone up the wall—especially the teacher."

Arthur Peake remembers also that the teacher at Athalmer always thought there was something special about the wood in their stove. The pupils had a habit of throwing cartridges into the stove when stoking it, and when the door was closed the Fourth of July celebration would start. "Such noisy wood!" the teacher would say. She would examine the woodpile closely and it seemed very normal, but definitely the wood was explosive!

Ink bottles, too, could be used for harassment. Mr. Hewat of Enderby attended Fairview School. He recalls pupils gathering around the stove on cold mornings, thawing

Stranby School on northern Vancouver Island, 1914.

out their ink bottles by rolling them around on their corners on top of the stove. It was more satisfying, however, to leave your ink bottle on the stove, tightly corked. The ceiling above the stove in Fairview school was covered with ink splashes, with little round clear spots in the middle where the corks had blown out.

But it was not just in the playing of pranks that children's imaginations excelled. Many were the games which pupils of these early schools invented, sports equipment being scarce or non-existent. Art Long, who attended Pallister School in the Bulkley Valley, remembers a form of hockey which the boys played:

"We formed a game of our own which was equivalent to hockey, only there was no ice. We ran on the snow. We had no pucks so we took the horses' hardwood singletrees and cut blocks off them and used them for pucks. We used crooked willow sticks for hockey sticks, and eventually we got around to making mallets. You take a block of hardwood about two and a half inches across and hit it with your mallet . . . with no shin pads on, it gets pretty rough. We got pretty involved in this game.

"One day the teacher came back from lunch and found Margaret Saunders lying in a snow bank and blood pouring from her eye. The game was going on as usual. We got a real strenuous lecture about sportsmanship. Well, we tried to explain to the teacher that we told her to go into the school, and she wouldn't go. She just lay in the snow bank and bled. That was too rough for the teacher. He couldn't cope with it!"

"Nobbies" was another remembered game of the time, somewhat resembling lacrosse, and depending on homemade equipment. Two spools or two chestnuts were threaded onto a leather thong, and thrown with a hooked stick. Numerous black eyes resulted until the ire of the power and telephone companies, whose lines in certain areas became festooned with "nobbies," outlawed the game.

Games played at the Brentwood School

Benvoulin School.

on Vancouver Island, which opened in 1880, were rough in the early days. Historian John Windsor talked to some old-timers who recalled kids carrying shotguns to school and shooting at each other with gravel and berries. Tree-topping was a great sport too. A boy would climb up forty or fifty feet and snap off the top of a tree. One pupil fell and was knocked unconscious, but was quickly doused with cold water and pushed into school semi-conscious.

One of the more acrobatic games played at Kitsumgallum School, near Terrace, is recalled by Frank Floyd. It was called "One, two, three, bucket." One team would line up and bend over with backs horizontal. While the lead man braced himself with his head against the school wall, the others would put their hands on their hips and ready themselves. First, one and then another of the enemy team would leap onto their backs. The first team would have to bear the whole weight of the second team long enough to yell in chorus, "One, two, three, bucket!" They were then able to collapse in a heap.

Buster Hamilton, who attended school at the 115 on the Cariboo road, recalls a game called "rocks." This was played constantly by all the kids, large and small. The equipment and rules were basic. The school was split and each side had a pile of rocks. Anyone smart enough to cross enemy lines and steal a rock brought it home. If caught, he remained a prisoner until freed. The game ended when one side had all the rocks.

Of course children played many of the old familiar games still played by some children today—"Red Rover, Red Rover," "Pom, Pom, Pullaway," "Run, Sheep, Run," "Duck on a Rock," "Anti, Anti-I-Over," and "Kick the Can." None of these games required expensive equipment, and all could be played by the whole school.

Most former pupils of rural school recall the excitement of the first snowfall and a game called "fox and geese." The older children would make sure no one tracked up the lovely white expanse of snow before recess-time. Then a huge circle was marked out, the centre being the fox's lair. Paths led out from the centre, like cuts in a pie, and the geese lined themselves up around the circumference, making runs through the centre and daring the fox to tag them. Caught geese had to stay in the fox's lair.

As soon as the snow melted in the spring, and as sure as the arrival of the robins, the never-ending game of "rounders" or "scrub" ball began. This was a form of ballgame that could be played by everyone. There were no sides, simply positions, with the pitcher being first position, catcher, second position, and so on through the bases. When the first fellow was caught out, he went to the outfield and worked his way up again. Everyone, even the smallest child, had a chance to bat and pitch.

When the Hilton School opened in 1907, near Cherry Creek in the Shuswap area, the wife of the man who built the school did her part by making the ball. She bound together strips from tire tubes and sewed leather casing over all. The bat was a discarded peevee handle.

Although games and pranks are a delight to remember, pupils of one-room schools also recall the very serious competition for Honour Rolls. These important-looking scrolls, which were given for "proficiency," "attendance," and "deportment" were usually presented at the school picnic in May or June, often causing the parents of the winners to be flushed with pleasure, while the parents of less successful children felt twinges of ill-concealed jealousy. Years later, these treasured scrolls turn up amongst a welter of snapshots, dog-eared school books, report cards, and drawings in the bottom of some trunk or box, still emanating an aura of great importance for the owner.

Although the earlier backwoods schools were far away from the great cultural centres of the world, and received important news only by the occasional letter or newspaper, a good teacher could open up vistas of ideas and events far beyond the limits of the children's small world.

Mr. D.W. Sutherland was the teacher of Kelowna's first school, which was held above a store at the corner of what are now Ellis and Queensway Streets. The Kelowna Historical Society records that a small six-year-old named Bud Weddell attended that school and remembered, when a grown man, a day of great significance. News had travelled down the lake, by means of the the officers of the steamship *Aberdeen*, of Queen Victoria's illness. No doubt Mr. Sutherland explained to his pupils the historic role of the British Empire, and showed them on a globe of the world the vast extent of pink area over which Queen Victoria reigned. As the *Aberdeen* pulled in on January 22, 1901, Mr. Sutherland put his head out of the high window of the school and noticed the ship's flag at half-mast.

Bud Weddell recalled the solemnity of the moment and the hush in the little schoolroom when Mr. Sutherland turned, with a pale face, and announced, "The Queen is dead."

Great thoughts and high ideals were often introduced to pupils in early schools through the literature in their readers. The *Canadian Fourth Reader*, used for Grades Seven and Eight, was published in 1916. The introduction states rather ponderously, "While it is not possible for pupils to carry away from the study of such selections all that maturer minds will find in them, there is no reason to doubt that even young people may be greatly impressed by the loftiness of thought, the felicity of diction, and the 'witchery of the consummate verse.'" So thoroughly were the selections in this book studied and committed to memory that many a grey-haired oldster, once launched, can recite poetry for hours. There were poems which recalled the romantic history of Canada:

> In the seaport of St. Malo, 'twas a smiling morn in May,
> When the commodore Jacques Cartier to the westward sailed away . . .

and

> Out and in the river is winding, the links of its long red chain,
> Through belts of dusky pineland and gusty leagues of plain.
> Only at times a smoke-wreath with the drifting cloud-rack joins
> The smoke of the hunting lodges of the wild Assiniboines.

There were solemn poems about the British Empire:

> God of our fathers, known of old,
> Lord of our far-flung battle line,
> Beneath whose awful hand we hold
> Dominion over palm and pine . . .

and there were some poems too sad for school children to understand:

> Break, break, break, on thy cold grey stones, oh sea . . .

Frank Floyd studied from this reader while attending a one-room school near Terrace in the early 1900s, and many of the poems still give him pleasure. A passage which he memorized while a Grade Seven student returned to him rather unexpectedly one day. He claims that he sat down to milk a certain cow by the name of May, and being in an expansive mood, said to the cow, "Well, May . . ." These two words triggered his memory, and he found himself reciting a whole soliloquy on the death of Samuel Johnson, which begins with the lines:

> Well may the world cherish his renown.
> His has been purchased not by deeds of violence or blood,
> But by the diligent dispensation of pleasure . . .

Memory can surprise us, bringing back with

sharpness and immediacy the emotions and sensations of childhood. Memory does not discriminate. While one person may recall prosaically a long list of the English kings and their dates, learned at school many years before, another may remember the peculiar but not unpleasant odor of grey slate pencils, or the smell of a freshly oiled school floor. Even flies buzzing in an outhouse can cause the mind to flash back to earlier school days.

More romantic is one pupil's memory of a damp and secret spot in the woods where she and her sisters lingered on the way to school to admire a patch of fragile pink ladyslippers . . . or Vera Campbell's memory of the lovely autumn smell of yellow and red cranberry bushes along the trail to Dragon Lake School.

Dr. Neil Morrison, who attended Deadwood School over sixty years ago, has a photograph of twenty-five grey-haired men and women who showed up at a reunion of that school. They are standing on a flat area close to the railway tracks which connected Greenwood smelter with the mother-lode mine—the exact site where the old school stood. Not a trace is left, however, of the cream-coloured frame building. It has vanished. Only the memories remain, and these were strong enough to bring back elderly people whose paths had diverged for over half a century.

Okanagan Mission School, 1894. The four Cosorso boys rode to school on an obliging and patient horse and other students jumped on along the trail.

Epilogue: The Teacher Returns

The forest is very still, and the scent of warm pine needles fills me with overwhelming nostalgia. I push my way through the thick underbrush, searching for the trail that winds through the dense jackpine forest to the school house. Few people use it now because there is no one left who remembers. . . .

Branches whip my face, and vines clutch at my clothing. At last the trees thin out, the sunlight intensifies, and I step into the clearing.

The school house still stands there, very much alone, surrounded by the dark encroaching forest.

Memories from nearly half a century ago flood back. The little clearing seems filled with ghostly voices of many children . . . high, thin voices which call and laugh, and then are still again.

The hot August sun shines down on the old building. Its logs are silver now, and some have sagged. The sod roof has caved in; yellow daisies grow on it, and tall brown grass. A blackberry vine climbs up one wall, over the broken windows, and nearly blocks the entrance to the little vestibule.

I step over the threshold and the door swings closed behind me, creaking on its one remaining hinge. The floor is littered with paper, and a strong odour of pack rat pervades the room. The blackboard is still on the wall, but the desks are gone, and so is the drum stove, although a section of rusted pipe hangs crazily from the ceiling. The scene is one of utter desolation. Impossible to believe that I, at twenty-one, stood on this very spot, teaching fourteen very real and lively children.

Suddenly, outside the window, a meadowlark trills its heartbreakingly beautiful song, and a gentle breeze sets all the aspen leaves aflutter. A shaft of sunlight falls across the room, and I imagine I see the children, shuffling and sighing in the drowsy warmth of the classroom, only half aware of my voice, and gazing longingly out of the window at the springtime world.

Joan Adams was born in Kelowna and spent ten years teaching in one-room schools in British Columbia and the Yukon. She returned to her birthplace to live after retiring in 1979.

Becky Thomas was born in Kelowna and also taught school before returning there to live. She and Joan Adams have been friends since childhood. Apart from one-room schools, their main interests are camping, horseback riding and hiking around B.C.

ISBN 0-920080-69-3
Jacket design by Ian Bateson
Jacket photograph by Chris Czartoryski
Interior design by Gaye Hammond
Typesetting by Baseline Type & Graphics
Printed & bound in Canada by D.W. Friesen & Sons

HARBOUR PUBLISHING CO. LTD.
MADEIRA PARK, B.C.